Big League Again

The 1970 Milwaukee Brewers

David Ellmann

ISBN-13: 9781648581717
ISBN-10: 1648581714

Cover image: Author's personal collection
By: David Ellmann for Design Associates

Acknowledgments

I have always been a baseball fan. Some of my earliest memories are ball games with my father and collecting baseball cards with the neighborhood kids. I went to my first game in 1970 and from that day on I was hooked. I've been fascinated with that first team that the Brewers fielded and the circumstances surrounding them. I'm not old enough to remember when the Braves were in Milwaukee so I do not understand the heartbreak that those fans must have felt. I do know that for the past 50 years I've loved my Milwaukee Brewers, and I don't think there are many things better than a warm summer's day at the ballpark.

This book started out as a research paper for a college course and as I delved into the story of the 1970 Milwaukee Brewers I became convinced that it was a compelling story that would make an interesting book. Tracking down the men that played on that first team was difficult, some dropped from sight, and sadly some had passed on. The ones I was able to contact were more than gracious with their time and I will be forever grateful that they shared their memories with me so I could pass them on to Brewers fans everywhere.

I would like to thank Dave Baldwin, Al Downing, Lew Krausse, Ted Kubiak, Bob Locker, Jerry Mc Nertney, Bob Meyer, John O'Donoghue, Rich Rollins, Phil Roof, Ken Sanders, Ted Savage, Wes Stock, and Floyd Wicker for taking the time to answer my questions and making this book possible.

For game and other information I found Google News Archives, newspapers.com, and Baseball Reference to be invaluable resources. Reading the newspaper accounts on a day-to-day basis was like stepping into a baseball time machine, gaining insight on not only the game, but the world in general in that era

The author at age two having a catch with his Dad

PROLOGUE

1970. America was reeling after the turbulent sixties and change was everywhere. There were still signs of the old guard, Richard Nixon was entering his second year as president, Jack Webb's Dragnet was wrapping up its second successful run on television, and Frank Sinatra was still doing it his way. Vietnam seemed to be the lead story on the nightly news as young Americans were still fighting and dying in Southeast Asia, while student protests continued to grow.

Change was coming and nowhere more rapidly than in professional sports. The American Football League played its last game on January 11th 1970 as the Kansas City Chiefs defeated the Minnesota Vikings in Super Bowl 4, ending a decade of rivalry with the NFL and leading up to a much-anticipated merger. Major League Baseball witnessed the New York Mets' stunning upset of the heavily favored Baltimore Orioles in the 1969 World Series, capping off a decade that saw one of the games most hallowed records broken, and the expansion of baseball into new markets. Baseball's attendance had been declining throughout the 1960s as the National Football League experienced tremendous growth in popularity, and expansion was looked at with some skepticism. The first round of expansion was as a result of franchise shifts, with a new team placed in Washington DC in response to the Senators move to Minnesota in 1961, and the National League Mets in 1962 as a replacement for the departed Giants and Dodgers. Franchises in Houston and Los Angeles rounded out the first round of expansion.

Baseball's second round of expansion can be traced back to Charles O. Finley's decision to move the Athletics from Kansas City to Oakland after the 1967 season. Missouri Senator Stuart Symington threatened to introduce legislation that would revoke Major League Baseball's antitrust exemption if Kansas City was not given a team to replace the departing A's. Not wanting to lose that exemption Major League Baseball agreed to expand, awarding teams to Kansas City, Seattle, Montreal, and San Diego, to begin play in 1971. Increasing pressure from Symington forced Major League Baseball to move that schedule up, leading to a series of events that created one of the most unique franchise situations in MLB history.

It was against this backdrop that a jilted community's appetite for baseball was finally satisfied, beginning a love affair with a team that continues to grow. This is the story of that first group of heroes and the rebirth of baseball in Milwaukee.

CHAPTER ONE

The City of Milwaukee has a rich baseball history dating back to the early days of the game. As far back as 1876 the city fielded an independent team called the West Ends. 1878 saw the formation of the Milwaukee Grays, also referred to as Brewers, as a member of an early incarnation of the National League. Milwaukee would be home to professional baseball sporadically over the next decade with teams competing in the Union Association, Western Association, and American Association, with none of the teams lasting more than a year or two.

In 1894 the Western League was formed and included the city of Milwaukee as one of the initial franchises. Initially operating as a minor league the Western League also fielded teams in Indianapolis, Kansas City, Cleveland, Toledo, and Omaha/ Keokuk Iowa. The league would be reorganized several times over the next few years finding the right balance of solid franchises. In 1897 the Brewers, as they were now known, made a deal with

Connie Mack to manage the team and act as an occasional backup catcher. Mack would go on to manage the team through the 1900 season before leaving to take the position of manager and later owner of the Philadelphia Athletics, where he would spend the next 50 years of his Hall of Fame career.

An historic event that would shape the face of baseball took place on the evening of March 5th 1900 at the Republican Hotel in Downtown Milwaukee, as five men gathered in room 185 and established what is now known as the American League. After playing one final season as a so-called minor league, the American League replaced several clubs with larger Eastern cities and became baseball's second Major League. Unfortunately for the City of Milwaukee the Brewers franchise was moved to the city of St Louis and renamed the Browns, where they would play until they moved to Baltimore in 1954.

Milwaukee was not without professional baseball very long as in 1902 the Milwaukee Brewers returned as a member of the minor-league American

Association. The Brewers were one of the most successful minor league teams and spent the next 51 years as a member of the American Association. The club won six American Association championships, in 1913, 1914, 1936, 1944, 1951, and 1952. Two of those teams, the 1944 club and 1952 team are ranked among the hundred greatest minor league teams of all time, with the 1944 club winning 102 games as a Double-A affiliate, and the 1952 squad winning 101 in their final season as a minor league team. That '44 Brewers season was noteworthy in that after manager Charlie Grimm left at the beginning of May to take over as manager of the Chicago Cubs, the Brewers hired the recently fired Casey Stengel to take over the club, and the team ran roughshod over their American Association opponents the remainder of the season. Stengel's managerial career prior to coming to Milwaukee had been unsuccessful to say the least and his winning seasons in Milwaukee were a springboard to resurrecting his managerial career with the "Old

Perfessor" eventually finding his way to New York City, and everyone knows what happened there.

In 1941 the club was purchased by Bill Veeck in a partnership with former Cub star Charlie Grimm. Under Veeck's ownership, the Brewers would become one of the most colorful squads in baseball and Veeck would become one of the game's premier showmen. Always on the lookout for new promotional gimmicks Veeck would giveaway live animals, schedule morning games for the wartime night shift workers, stage weddings at home plate and once sent manager Grimm a birthday cake containing a much-needed left-handed pitcher. Veeck initially balked at Grimm's suggestion of Casey Stengel as his replacement but as Veeck was stationed overseas in the Marine Corps, Grimm won out and Stengel got the job. In 1945, after winning three American Association pennants in five years, Bill Veeck sold his interest in the Brewers for a $275,000 profit. Veeck would not be out of baseball long, resurfacing as owner of the Cleveland Indians in 1946. He would later own the St. Louis Browns, at one point attempting to move the team to Milwaukee for the 1953 season, and would also own the Chicago White Sox on two separate occasions.

During their entire 51 year tenure in the American Association the Milwaukee Brewers played in the same ballpark. Borchert Field was originally constructed in 1888 and was located on the north side of Milwaukee on a rectangular city block. With its main entrance on Chambers Street between 8th and 9th Streets its location in the middle of the urban neighborhood led to an oddly-shaped playing field. The foul lines were abnormally short, 268 ft. to left and right field respectively, with fences that angled sharply making for deep power alleys, with center field being four hundred feet from home plate. With a maximum capacity of 12,000 fans and the oddly-shaped playing field, the ballpark was an intimate setting to watch baseball. Lights were added to the park in 1935 and a 1944 windstorm tore off a portion of the first base grandstand roof. By that time, taking into account the age of the ballpark and its deteriorating condition the roof was never replaced. By the late 1940's Borchert Field was the oldest park in the American Association and was becoming ramshackle and dilapidated. The park's residential location provided virtually no parking for the fans that by now preferred to take their automobiles to the game as opposed to public transportation. By this time the city fathers in Milwaukee had undertaken the task of securing financing to build a new ballpark for the Brewers in hopes of attracting a major league team to Milwaukee once again.

As far back as the 1930's city leaders considered the idea of a new ballpark to house not only baseball but professional football as well. Several sites were considered, an area at 35th and Oklahoma, the Wisconsin State Fair Park grounds, and the north side of Milwaukee not far from where Borchert Field stood. The city finally settled on the defunct site of the Story Quarry, on the west side of Milwaukee near the Story Hill neighborhood. Ground was broken on October 19th 1950, and although hampered by steel shortages due to the

Korean War, Milwaukee's new baseball palace was set to open at the beginning of the 1953 season. Constructed at a cost of $5.9 million dollars the newly-christened Milwaukee County Stadium was the first ballpark in the United States to be financed with public funds and the first to be built surrounded by a parking lot. With an initial capacity of 36,011 the Brewers new home would be the crown jewel of the American Association and would be ready to host a major league franchise when one became available. That day would come much quicker than anyone could have possibly imagined!

The Brewers would never play a game in the home that was initially built for them. The team at the time was a Triple A affiliate of the Boston Braves, and their owner Lou Perini was eyeing the City of Milwaukee and their shiny new stadium as a future home for his struggling franchise. Playing second fiddle to the more popular Red Sox in Boston, the Braves were stuck in an aging ballpark, playing before a dwindling fan base. After drawing less than 280,000 fans for the 1952 season Perini sought permission to move his Braves to Milwaukee on March 13th 1953. Five days later the move was approved and Milwaukee had a major league baseball team for the first time since 1901.

To say that Milwaukee and its citizens embraced the Braves would be an understatement. This was a full-fledged love affair from the beginning and the entire town was giddy with enthusiasm. The team was greeted as genuine heroes and did not disappoint, as the team won 92 games and finished in second place in their inaugural season. The fans did not disappoint either as 1,826,397 baseball crazy Milwaukeeans made their way to County Stadium setting a new National League attendance record, which they promptly proceeded to break the following year. Dubbed "The Miracle of Milwaukee", all of Major League Baseball paid attention as fans streamed into Milwaukee County Stadium in record numbers. So stunning were the attendance figures being set by the Braves that by the end of the decade the Browns, Athletics, Giants, and Dodgers all followed the Braves lead and pulled up stakes, heading for greener pastures and looking for that next "Miracle ".

The Braves were legitimate pennant contenders their first seven years in Milwaukee, winning the pennant in '57 and '58, and a World Series title in 1957 defeating the New York Yankees four games to three. They came within a game of the National League pennant in 1956, and in 1959 lost a three game playoff to the Los Angeles Dodgers for the National League pennant. From 1954 to 1957 the Braves routinely drew more than 2 million fans per season, which were outstanding numbers in those days and still pretty good in some markets today. By the end of the decade though the fans were getting spoiled and merely a winning record was not enough. Attendance began to decline and by 1962 the Braves struggled to draw a little over 750,000 fans. The sale of the team to a syndicate headed by Bill Bartholomay stoked rumors of a possible move from Milwaukee. The team's attendance improved a little bit in 1963 to 790,000, and even more in 1964 when the team drew 900,000.

By this time the rumors were more rampant and after the 1964 season it was confirmed. The Braves would be moving to Atlanta.

Like jilted lovers, both sides tried to inflict as much hurt on the other side, and the ugly breakup played out over the course of the 1965 season. Team owners offered Milwaukee County $500,000 to buy out the final year of their contract at County Stadium and were promptly refused, forcing the Braves to remain in Milwaukee for one more lame duck season. In spite of the acrimony and rumors swirling around the club the team still managed to play inspired baseball, so much so that they were in the race for the National League pennant through August before falling back to a fifth place finish. The team drew only 555,584 spectators, and considering the atmosphere surrounding the team it's amazing that many people showed up. The last home game was an 11 inning 7 - 6 loss to the Dodgers on September 22nd. 12,577 Milwaukee baseball fans turned out to say goodbye to the Braves. The Miracle of Milwaukee was over.

The next few seasons saw a handful of games played at County Stadium, with a Monday night exhibition game between the White Sox and the Twins drawing more than 51,000 fans, which was an incredible achievement considering County Stadium held 43,768 in those days. The White Sox would return to play nine "home" games in Milwaukee in 1968 and another 11 in 1969, easily out distancing their per game attendance figures in Chicago. The architect behind those games was former Braves minority owner Bud Selig, who was actively searching for a new team to call Milwaukee home. The attendance for those games showed Major League Baseball that Milwaukee was deserving of a team to call their own.

CHAPTER TWO

The Seattle Pilots were born out of Kansas City Athletics owner Charles O. Finley's decision to move his team to Oakland. After years of battling local Kansas City politicians Finley was done with the city and decided to pull up stakes in search of greener pastures. Charlie O initially considered moving the Athletics to Seattle due to the city's rich baseball tradition and its beautiful port center location. Finley loved the city, but he hated the existing Sicks' Stadium, calling it a "pigpen" and saying it was aptly named. After 30 years Sicks' Stadium was showing signs of wear and tear and was not aging well. Ultimately Finley chose Oakland as his team's new destination, but his decision set off a chain of events that would lead to excitement for Seattle's baseball fans and ultimately despair.

Finley's decision angered many back in Kansas City, most notably Missouri Senator Stuart Symington. Symington threatened Major League

Baseball that if the state's biggest city did not get a team to replace the A's, he was going to introduce legislation that would revoke the league's antitrust exemption, which would also challenge the reserve clause - a clause that kept players under contractual control by the team. The owners knew that their backs were against the wall, but they had no choice. They were not about to give up the reserve clause so they awarded Kansas City a new team - the Royals. In order to keep an even amount of teams in the American League (which the Royals would be joining) baseball decided to add an additional team. After much consideration they chose the third largest city in the West and an ownership group backed by former Seattle Rainier general manager Dewey Soriano and former Cleveland Indians owner William Daley. Seattle had long been a hotbed for minor league baseball and was home to the Seattle Rainiers, one of the pillars of the Pacific Coast League (PCL). The Cleveland Indians had almost moved to Seattle in 1965 and many of the same things that attracted the Indians made Seattle a plum choice for an expansion team. Seattle was the third-biggest metropolitan area on the West Coast and their new team would be called the Pilots, and were slated to begin play in 1971.

Senator Symington was still not satisfied. Reneging on an earlier agreement that the teams would begin played during the 1971 season, over three years from the original agreement, Symington wanted a team playing in Kansas City as soon as possible. Once again Major League Baseball was trying to appease the politicians and revised their earlier decision. The new American League franchises in Kansas City and Seattle, along with National League franchises in Montreal and San Diego would begin play in April of 1969. Ready or not the city of Seattle had Major League Baseball coming in 18 months. Major League Baseball immediately placed conditions upon the city and the team owners that needed to be met by Opening Day 1969. The first thing that the city needed to do was to update Sicks' Stadium and bring it up to Major League standards. At the time the stadium only had seats for 11,000 fans and the MLB wanted the stadium to seat a minimum of thirty thousand. Long-term, Major League Baseball wanted a domed stadium in Seattle and demanded that construction start by December 31st 1970. Also, the Pilots had to pay the PCL $1 million to compensate for the loss of one of its most successful franchises. After King County voters approved a bond for a domed stadium (what would become the Kingdome) in February 1968 with 62% in favor, the Seattle Pilots were officially born. California Angels executive Marvin Milkes was hired as general manager, and Joe Schultz, a coach with the National League Champion St. Louis Cardinals, became manager

With such a short period of time to meet Major League Baseball's demands the city of Seattle scrambled to get the stadium in shape. After much haggling the owners convinced baseball to reduce the number of seats required to 25,000, yet the project still went way over budget causing additional agreements to be made in order to get anywhere close to the original budget. The owners settled for less costly lighting, the smallest possible restrooms that would pass code, interior walls made out of plywood, and no built-in utilities for the concession stands as just some of the cost-cutting measures. Despite that, the stadium still wouldn't be ready on Opening Day as workmen were still installing seats as fans were entering the stadium.

The Pilots' owners wanted to field a competitive team immediately and that eagerness showed when it came time for the expansion draft. Held on October 15th 1968 the American League version of the expansion draft featured two different philosophies. The Royals decided to go with younger players that they could develop while the Pilots chose to go the veteran route, selecting more experienced players and former All-Stars. Drafting players such as Don Mincher, Tommy Harper, Gary Bell, Tommy Davis, Jim Bouton, and Steve Barber stocked the roster with names that the fans would recognize, but for the most part they would never regain their former All Star levels.

The team chose blue and gold as their colors and although the uniforms were extremely popular with the fans they were less well received by the players. The home whites featured blue and gold Captain's trim on the sleeves, a patch with a captain's wheel and wings, and the team name in lowercase letters. The road uniforms were powder blue with the same trim on the sleeves and Seattle in a combination of upper and lowercase letters on the jersey front. Both uniforms featured a navy blue cap with a giant gold S, along with gold braids on the crown, and as the military called them 'scrambled eggs" on the bill. Pitcher Jim Bouton wrote in his book Ball Four that *the uniforms made the players look like goddamn clowns*. Say what you will about the uniforms they certainly were a departure from the typical styles of the day in Major League Baseball.

With a roster of experienced veteran players Schultz and Milkes both optimistically stated that they thought Pilots could finish third in the newly formed, six-team AL West. However, the Pilots experienced the typical struggles of a first-year expansion team. They won their very first game, and then their home opener three days later, but only won five more times in the first month. Nevertheless, the Pilots managed to stay in reasonable striking distance of .500, at least through June, and were only 6 games back of the division lead as late as June 28. But a disastrous 9–20 July (and an even worse 6–22 August) ended even a faint hope of any kind of contention, though they were still in third place as late as August. The team finished the season in last place in the AL West with a record of 64-98, 33 games out of first (Minnesota), and 45 games behind league-leading Baltimore.

Despite their Opening Day win, the pressure on the team and the stadium was great in the spring of 1969. Not only were they playing in an unfinished substandard stadium, the Pilots ticket prices were among the highest in baseball. Those facts combined with the team's ineptitude on the field did not sit well with the fans. The team's poor play was the least of its troubles. The most glaring problem was the stadium itself. Sicks' Stadium was the longtime home of the PCL's Seattle Rainiers and was once considered one of the best ballparks in minor league baseball. By 1969 however it was considered obsolete and behind the times. Although one of the conditions of Major League Baseball awarding in the franchise to Seattle was that the stadium had to be expanded to 30,000 seats, later reduced to 25,000, only 19,500 seats were ready by Opening Day because of numerous construction delays. The stadium also suffered from many other issues. The scoreboard was not ready until the night before the season opener, and it took until June before there were finally 25,000 seats available. Water pressure in the stadium was so bad that toilets couldn't be flushed during games and was almost non-existent after the seventh inning, especially with crowds above 8,000. In addition, the visiting team's announcers couldn't see plays along third base or left field. The Pilots had to place a mirror in the press box, and visiting broadcasters were forced to look into it and "refract" plays in those areas. The Pilots total attendance for 1969 was 677,944, an average of

8,268, which ranked 20th out of 24 teams, ahead of only the Cleveland Indians, the Chicago White Sox the Philadelphia Phillies and expansion San Diego Padres. The other two expansion teams outdrew the Pilots, with the Kansas City Royals drawing 902,414 spectators, and the Montreal Expos who surprised everyone by finishing 10th in attendance with 1,212,600 paid admissions. The Pilots largest crowd was 23,657 on August 3rd for a game against the New York Yankees, while the lowest attendance for a home game was that April 29th 1969 when a paltry 1,954 fans showed up to watch them play the California Angels .

The franchise began hemorrhaging money quickly and the bickering between Major League Baseball, the Pilots and the city of Seattle increased. By the end of September as the team was losing more than they were winning, owner William Daley told the public that if they didn't start coming to games he would move the team. The City of Seattle, trying to blame the ownership group, said that if the team didn't pay their bills (they were renting Sicks'

Stadium from the city) that they would evict them immediately. Needless to say the very public threats between the city and the team did not sit well with the fans, and during the final month of the season attendance dropped to roughly forty-five hundred people on average per game. There were also concerns that the team would not be able to make payroll, although it appears they never missed a payday, and such an action could have plunged a franchise into chaos. The team was able to limp through until the end of the season and was faced with an offseason of serious questions about the future of the franchise.

The franchise was undercapitalized from the start and the scramble was on to find investors to shore up the precarious financial situation. As fall turned into winter, and winter into spring the team's finances were in ruins and it was clear that something would need to be done. The team had an official theme song, "Go,Go, You Pilots", and go, go they did. First to Bankruptcy Court, and then 1,900 miles to the east. But not before an interesting offseason.

CHAPTER THREE

The Milwaukee White Sox? This may sound far-fetched today, but in the summers of 1968 and 1969 this was closer to reality than most think.

When it appeared that the Braves would be heading south to Atlanta, Milwaukee native and long-time baseball fan Bud Selig began organizing local movers and shakers to oppose the move. By July of 1965 when it was certain that the Braves would be leaving, Selig christened his group Milwaukee Brewers Baseball Club Incorporated and began the quest to return baseball to Milwaukee. The group would need to move fast because in 1967, both major leagues had voted to expand.

To show the viability of Milwaukee as a Major League market Selig's group staged a Monday night exhibition game between the Chicago White Sox and the Minnesota Twins at Milwaukee County Stadium. More than 51,000 fans turned out. Taking into account that County Stadium only held 43,768 in those days it was a remarkable feat, especially for a game that did not count in the standings. Although both clubs were from bordering states it's safe to assume that the majority of fans in attendance were local. The fact that his group was able to talk both teams into spending a day off playing an exhibition game in Milwaukee is a feat in and of itself and to draw a standing-room-only crowd makes it even more amazing. While the game was a nice showcase for the City of Milwaukee and their hopes of regaining Major League Baseball, it also shed light on the White Sox' plight on the south side of Chicago.

For the previous decade-and-a-half the White Sox routinely outdrew the crosstown Cubs in the grandstands and outplayed them on the field. From 1951 to 1966 the White Sox never fell below .500, while in that same time period the Cubs only finished in the first division once. It would seem that the White Sox' domination at the gate would continue well into the future. But something strange was going on in the Windy City.

The summer of 1967 saw the White Sox locked in an epic battle with the Red Sox, Tigers, and

Twins for the American League pennant. The South Siders led this close race for 2 and 1/2 months, with all four teams being tied for first place at the beginning of September. The Sox were in the race the final week of the season, eventually finishing three games behind the "Impossible Dream" Red Sox. Despite the excitement of the wild pennant race a funny thing happened. The fans didn't support the team as expected. A pivotal four-game weekend Series against the Detroit Tigers from September 8th - 10th drew a total of 60,000 fans, while just four days later a cozy gathering of 4,314 watched the White Sox defeat the Cleveland Indians. *Chicago Tribune* sportswriter Edward Prell stated what many were thinking: *"In their moment of triumph, the White Sox have cause to wonder what's happened to their fans."* In fact, even though the White Sox almost won the pennant their attendance actually declined in 1967

There were several factors involved in the White Sox dismal attendance in spite of being a pennant contender. The Sox played their home games on Chicago's South Side at White Sox Park (

also known as Comiskey Park), and the surrounding neighborhood was beginning to decline and was thought to be unsafe by some fans. The team's style of play was also considered dull by some fans as the team relied on ground balls and strikeouts and played in what was considered the worst hitters park in baseball. A bigger factor was the resurgence of the crosstown rival Chicago Cubs. The Cubs were awakening from years of inept play, and now under the guiding hand of Leo Durocher featured an exciting team with future Hall of Famers Ernie Banks, Billy Williams, Ron Santo, and Fergie Jenkins.

It was against this backdrop that White Sox owner Arthur Allyn agreed to a proposal by Bud Selig for the White Sox to stage nine home games - not exhibition games- in Milwaukee in 1968. Although it was not unprecedented for a team to play at an alternate location, White Sox fans had to be somewhat alarmed. All they had to do was look back a decade earlier, and recall that the Brooklyn Dodgers had played "home" games in Jersey City in

1956 and 1957 before abandoning Brooklyn for Los Angeles.

These games in Milwaukee would serve as a reminder to Major League Baseball that Milwaukee County Stadium was still only 15 years old, and was ready to accept one of the new expansion teams, and serve as a showcase for the city's support of baseball. Any hopes Milwaukee had of landing one of the new expansion franchises were dashed on May 27th 1968 when the National League announced that Montreal and San Diego would join the league the following season. In the American League Kansas City was already given, and the other franchise was awarded to the city of Seattle. This turn of events further stoked the rumor mills that the White Sox were not long for Chicago and would soon migrate north to the Brew City.

The plan for 1968 was for each American League team to play the White Sox one time at County Stadium in Milwaukee. All the games were scheduled for weeknights and would either be the first or last game of the series. While the results on the field for the White Sox were dismal, they would only go 1 - 8 and were shut out four times, the team's performance at the box office was another story, as a grand total of 264,478 fans showed up for the nine games scheduled at County Stadium, with an average crowd of 29,366 per game. On the flip side the White Sox only drew 539,478 paying customers to White Sox Park for the other 72 games for an average of slightly more than 7,500 per game. When you take into account that almost one-third of their home attendance occurred in those nine games in Milwaukee it's easy to see that the White Sox were ripe for relocation.

The gaudy attendance figures for the White Sox "home on the road" games made it easier for owner Arthur Allyn to bring the White Sox back to Milwaukee again in 1969. Once again each American League team would play one week day game in Milwaukee, and thanks to expansion this time there would be 11 games at County Stadium. This time the White Sox played winning baseball in Milwaukee, winning seven and losing four in the eleven games they played. Although attendance was down in both Milwaukee and Chicago in 1969, the percentage of the fans attending games in Milwaukee was even greater than the year before. Of the 589,546 fans who attended White Sox games in 1969 391,335 did so at White Sox Park, for an average of 6,673 while 198,211 attended games in Milwaukee, for an average of 18,019 fans per game. Looking at these figures you can see the average attendance at Milwaukee County Stadium was almost three times the average attendance at White Sox Park. Considering the White Sox only drew an Opening Day crowd of a little over 7,700 the season following that tremendous pennant race show the dire straits at the franchise was in.

Having been left out in the last round of expansion Selig's group turned their attention towards acquiring the White Sox. By this point in time there was no other choice to bring baseball back to Milwaukee, and the 20 games that the White Sox played the past two seasons in Milwaukee showed that the city could more than support Major

League Baseball once again. Unfortunately the American League owners did not want to abandon the large Chicago market and the deal was essentially killed when owner Arthur Allyn sold the team to his brother John, who was against moving the team out of Chicago. The sale had to be a devastating blow to Selig and his group after all the hard work that went into staging the games the past two seasons. Little did they know that the game on June 16th between the White Sox and the Pilots would be a harbinger of things to come.

1968 White Sox "Home" games in Milwaukee,

May 15	Angels 4 - White Sox 2	23,510
May 29	Orioles 3 - White Sox 2	18,748
June 17	White Sox 2 - Indians 1	28,081
June 24	Twins 1 - White Sox 0	25,267
July 11	Yankees 5 - White Sox 4	40,575
July 22	Athletics 4 - White Sox 0	30,818
Aug. 8	Red Sox 1 - White Sox 0	33,872
Aug. 21	Tigers 3 - White Sox 0	42,808

1969 White Sox "Home" games in Milwaukee

April 23	White Sox 7 - Angels 1	8,565
May 22	White Sox 7 - Tigers 3	15,948
May 28	White Sox 7 - Yankees 6	16,749
June 11	White Sox 4 - Indians 3	15,715
June 16	White Sox 8 - Pilots 3	13,133
July 2	Twins 4 - White Sox 2	23,525
July 7	White Sox 2 - Athletics 0	26,659
Aug. 6	Senators 4 - White Sox 3	25,520

Aug. 13	White Sox 5 - Red Sox 3	24,708
Sept. 1	Orioles 8 - White Sox 0	18,102
Sept. 26	Royals 5 - White Sox 3	9,587

CHAPTER FOUR

Heading into the 1969 offseason the Pilots were a financial disaster. Due to the deteriorating state of Sicks' Stadium and the poor play of the team, Soriano had lost several hundred thousand dollars. Major shareholder Daley had refused to invest any more money in the team especially since a new stadium was still years away. Even if the Pilots could hold on until the new stadium was built it was another issue that complicated matters even more.

That issue was with a company called SportService, a Minneapolis-based food distribution company. SportsService had been the chief provider of concessions for Major League Baseball for decades, and it staked 2 million dollars to the Pilots contingent on becoming the team's concession company. The problem with that is that Seattle law at the time prevented any public building - like the proposed domed stadium which the Pilots were desperate to move to once construction was finished - from selecting a concessionaire without undergoing the required competitive bidding process. At the time Dewey Soriano was known to have told a SportService representative, *"If we can't put you in that dome, we recognize we might have to go someplace else."* It's difficult to know if that hurdle could have been overcome when Seattle's new domed stadium, the Kingdome, was completed in 1976, but it's questionable if the Pilots could have even survived that long anyways considering the desperate condition of their current ballpark.

Rumors were circulating as far back as August of 1969 that the Pilots would be leaving for Dallas-Fort Worth for the 1970 season, but Texas millionaire and Kansas City Chiefs owner Lamar Hunt, who himself had been seeking a major league team of his own denied those reports. Yet by late September Hunt presented Daley, the Pilots chairman of the board, an offer to purchase the club, but surprisingly Daley rejected the offer insisting that the franchise would be staying in Seattle. When the season ended though, Pilots' president Dewey Soriano revealed that the team had lost over

$300,000 in its first season and that the Pilots were for sale and listening to all potential suitors.

One of those suitors, Bud Selig, had everything in place, investors, a Major League ready stadium, and a city dying for a new team. Fresh off the success of the White Sox "home away from home" games in 1968 and 1969 at County Stadium, Milwaukee appeared to be the logical choice for the struggling Pilots. Once Selig revealed his interest in purchasing the Pilots negotiations moved quickly and according to later testimony Selig used a handshake agreement during the eighth inning of game one of the 1969 World Series the purchase the Pilots for 10.8 million dollars. Considering that Soriano and Co. had purchased the team for just 5.3 million dollars a year earlier, the Milwaukee groups' offer had to be considered a godsend. It was also probably the worst kept secret around as 9 days later on October 20th, Chicago Daily News editor John P Carmichael said that the Pilots would move to Milwaukee for the 1970 season and play as the Milwaukee Brewers, and be owned by a Milwaukee-based group. He claimed that "Milwaukee has virtually sewed up the franchise." The next day, Leonard Koppett of the New York Times said that the owners meeting in Chicago would consider the "final" steps of moving the club to Milwaukee. Daley told reporters that he "would be happy to come to Milwaukee, if we could get permission from the American League." That move would require three-quarters of the 12 American League clubs to approve.

Once again things would not come easy for the Milwaukee group as the American League rejected this idea and required Seattle and the Pilots to work things out, partly by continuing to enlarge Sicks' Stadium and make additional improvements. Although the initial agreement was that construction of a domed stadium was to begin by the end of 1970, that did not seem to be anywhere near a reality.

With the club's ownership situation in limbo the front office still needed to continue with day-to-day operations while things were sorted out. In early November general manager Marvin Milkes dismissed the entire coaching staff, and several weeks later he fired manager Joe Schultz. Schultz his replacement, Dave Bristol, was the polar opposite of what the players were used to from their manager. Schultz was a veteran, easy going type who seemed to be able to keep the players in the clubhouse loose. While many of the players respected him, Jim Bouton said of Schultz in his book Ball Four, *"I think Joe Schultz knows the guys get a kick out of the funny and nonsensical things he says, so he says them deliberately. . .There's a zany quality to Joe Schultz that we all enjoy and that contributes, I believe, to keeping the club loose."*, some players thought that his likeable personna ultimately cost him his job. His replacement was a direct contrast. Bristol was young , only 36 when he was hired, and had just spent 3 ½ successful seasons at the helm of a young and rising Cincinnati Reds squad that was on the verge of becoming the "Big Red Machine". While Schultz was relaxed and easy going, Bristol was a no nonsense manager who expected maximum effort. Milkes' hiring of Bristol no doubt made a statement to the players but at the same time he made a statement to the doubters. At Bristol's introductory press conference Milkes told reporters *" I want to assure the baseball world and Pacific Northwest fans that this will be a stable organization and we can expect to see Major League Baseball here for many years to come."* Whether this was actually the true sentiment or just posturing we will never know, it at least created the illusion that things were business as usual.

Milkes may have had reason to believe that the Pilots would be staying in the Pacific Northwest, because as they were introducing Bristol as the new manager, the club had hopes that they had found its new owner in a group led by local businessman Fred Danz. The American League owners would decide in December if Danz would assume majority control of the team, while in the meantime Danz met with Seattle Mayor Wes Uhlman and agreed to provide the city with a $600,000 letter of credit and a $150,000 performance bond. There was one problem though. The money that Danz and hoped to receive to purchase the franchise was not immediately forthcoming, and Daley and Soriano brothers would remain in charge. In January 1970, Westin Hotels head Eddie Carlson put together a nonprofit group to buy the team. However, the owners of the other major league teams rejected the idea almost out of hand, since it would have devalued the other clubs' worth. A slightly modified deal came one vote short of approval. The club needed to raise $3.5 million dollars to remain afloat, and was given until January 22nd 1970 by the American League to make good on its finances. After missing the deadline, Mayor Uhlman threatened legal action if the Pilots were to leave Seattle. Mayor Tommy Vandergriff of Arlington Texas offered to expand and upgrade the minor-league Turnpike Stadium to bring it up to Major League standards, while Lamar Hunt continued to seek the franchise.

While all this was going on Selig and his Milwaukee investors were left in limbo as the Pilots status was resolved. It would not be a stretch to imagine the frustration that the group felt and the nagging thought that they could be once again shut out in their quest to return baseball to Milwaukee.

With spring training just around the corner there were still many unanswered questions.

CHAPTER FIVE

As 1969 turned into 1970 the Pilots' future looked bleaker by the day. Although they missed Major League Baseball's imposed deadline of January 22nd to get their finances in order, there was hope the franchise could remain in Seattle and Milkes still had a team to run. The general manager would jettison almost a dozen players from the 1969 squad through trades, acquiring several players who would play a major role in 1970. Perhaps his biggest deal occurred on January 15th as a six player swap with the Oakland Athletics netted first baseman Mike Hershberger, starting pitcher Lew Krausse, catcher Phil Roof, and relief pitcher Ken Sanders in exchange for first baseman Don Mincher and shortstop Ron Clark. The trade was a homecoming of sorts for Roof as he began his career with the Milwaukee Braves, appearing briefly in 1961 and again in 1964. Krausse and Sanders would both play big roles in 1970 and beyond and were huge upgrades to the club's pitching staff. Earlier additions of starting pitcher Bob Bolin and second baseman Ted Kubiak brought the club additional everyday players in exchange for what were essentially spare parts. As a matter of fact, the franchise as a whole was not without talent. Their minor league system boasted over a dozen players that would someday reach the Major Leagues including several who would have long and productive major league careers.

The Pilots were especially excited about top prospect, right-hander Miguel Fuentes. The 23 year old Fuentes was signed as an amateur free agent prior to the 1969 season and dazzled the Midwest League with the Clinton Pilots. Posting an 8 and 2 record in 26 appearances with a sparkling 1.46 ERA Fuentes earned a call up to the big club in September of '69. After making two relief appearances he was given his first start and responded by throwing a complete game against the Chicago White Sox, giving up one run on seven hits. Fuentes would start three other games before closing out the season with a relief appearance in the Pilot's final contest of 1969. Although he only posted a 1-3 mark with an

ERA over 5.00 he flashed enough promise that the club was expecting big things from him in 1970. During the MLB off-season in the winter of 1969 and 1970, Fuentes played in the Puerto Rican Winter League with the Caguas Criollos, looking to build on a successful first professional campaign, and prepare to compete for a spot on the big league roster in 1970. Sadly tragedy struck as a few days after the Criollos' season ended in the league's playoffs, on January 29, Fuentes was shot at a bar in Loíza Aldea. Fuentes had gone outside to relieve himself because there was a plumbing problem in the bathroom. Someone who thought Fuentes was doing it too close to his car shot him. Fuentes was shot three times and sent to a hospital in a state of shock where he died of his wounds shortly thereafter. For an organization that was dealing with so much uncertainty the shock of Fuentes' senseless murder cast a further pall over the off-season.

In February as the Pilots players and baseball operations staff prepared to report to camp in Tempe, Arizona for spring training, the American

League decided to keep the club under its current ownership and advanced it $650,000 to cover operating costs. Roy Hamey, former general manager of the Yankees, was selected by the American League to oversee the Pilots, though Milkes would remain in his role as general manager. With the uncertainty swirling around the club ticket sales were going nowhere near as well as the club officials hoped they would, yet Milkes said the notion of a potential Milwaukee move was "absolutely ridiculous."

As the club reported to spring training it appeared that the Pilots owners had reached an agreement on March 8th in which the Milwaukee group headed by Selig and Judge Robert Cannon would purchase the Pilots franchise for $9.5 million, with the team shifting to Milwaukee for the 1970 season. The enthusiasm was short lived as the State of Washington and the City of Seattle filed for a temporary restraining order preventing the sale and move of the franchise. It was clear not only to the other American League owners, but the players as well, that the Seattle franchise was dying from their financial ills. Rumors were flying during spring training among the players with a feeling of uncertainty as well. The players weren't sure where they would be playing and more importantly when or if they were even going to get paid. By mid-March the team lost the ability to use their spring training facility, having failed to comply with the agreements for the usage of the facilities. The facilities owner eventually ended up allowing day-to-day usage, even though the club was behind $500,000 to the facility.

With the situation getting worse by the day, the American League scheduled a meeting for March 17th in Tampa to examine the club's financial situation. Even before the meeting took place it was clear to the owners that the club could not survive any longer and the only solution was to move the franchise. On March 19, citing debts of $7.4 million, the Pilots owners requested that the team be sold to Milwaukee under the provisions of the Bankruptcy Act. While the American League owners were set to vote on the move at the Tampa meeting Eighth

Florida Circuit Court judge issued an order blocking any vote on the franchise move until the hearing could be held. Additionally, two other restraining orders in the State of Washington had been filed, one by the city and state, and another by a Seattle taxpayer which would prevent any move.

On March 26 a Federal bankruptcy referee set aside the restraining orders allowing the American League to vote on acceptance of Milwaukee as a member, but the transfer of the Seattle franchise would only be allowed if approved by the court. This effectively prevented any further action in the King County Superior Court of the earlier restraining actions filed.

Although nothing had been officially announced yet the players and staff were getting the feeling that they may be heading to Wisconsin instead of Washington as the team broke camp. Not everybody found out in the same manner though. Pitcher Dave Baldwin recalls, *"I first became aware of the move to Milwaukee when I came onto the field one morning and saw that a cardboard sign reading "Milwaukee" had been taped over "Seattle" on the scoreboard. That was about three or four days before when we were to leave our spring training facilities in Tempe."* With the move still up in the air the players had to scramble to make living arrangements, while the club had to decide where to send their equipment. With the team's finances in ruins and the Pilots' fate still undecided they sent their equipment truck from Tempe to Provo, Utah. Once there the drivers stopped and waited for word whether to continue on to Seattle or head northeast to Milwaukee.

The drivers would not have to wait long. At the bankruptcy hearing a week later, general manager Marvin Milkes testified there was not enough money to pay the coaches, players and office staff. Had Milkes been more than 10 days late in paying the players, they would have all become free agents and left Seattle without a team for the 1970 season. With this in mind, Federal Bankruptcy Referee Sidney Volinn declared the Pilots bankrupt and on the evening of March 31, the bankruptcy court ruled that

Daley and the Soriano brothers could sell their franchise to Selig's Milwaukee group for $10.8 million. The timing of the ruling was fortuitous as the purchase agreement signed by the Milwaukee investors on March 8 would have expired at 10:00 AM on April 1. The news had to have been a relief to the players living with the uncertainty during spring training. Pitcher Ken Sanders remembers *"We were told to be in the hotel ballroom at 10:00 PM. Five guys came into the room and Marty Pattin turned to me and said 'Jerry Lewis bought the team!' in reference to Bud Selig's resemblance to the legendary comedian."*

The years of hard work and heartbreak finally paid off for Bud Selig and his group of investors. Major League Baseball would be returning to Milwaukee once again! There was still much work to be done as Opening Day was only seven days away and although they finally had a team there was still a myriad details to be ironed out such as uniforms, tickets, etc. and not much time to get it done. But with the drive and perseverance shown to finally bring a team to Milwaukee there's no doubt that the newly minted Brewers organization would be ready to go on April 7.

CHAPTER SIX

Milwaukeeans awoke on the morning of April 1st to a banner headline in the Milwaukee Sentinel that read 'REFEREE OK'S PILOTS SALE, BASEBALL TO RETURN HERE". It couldn't have been considered a huge surprise; rumors started flying as early as September of the previous year that the Pilots franchise would be relocating to Milwaukee. So sure were some local television stations that they were reporting the Pilots spring training scores as if it was already a done deal and the team was Milwaukee's. But still, after all the up and downs experienced by Bud Selig and his investment group, seeing the confirmation in print made it seem real to the Milwaukee baseball fans that waited so long for a team to replace the departed Braves. The Milwaukee Brewers were real!

As hard as it was for Milwaukee baseball fans it had to be equally as difficult for the players. After going through the uncertainty of the club situation during spring training, the players were relieved that the situation was resolved and they knew where they would be playing that season. Milwaukee Sentinel writer Lou Chapman related the players' feelings in his April 1st column. The reactions of two players, infielder Ted Kubiak and pitcher George Lauzerique were indicative of the player's sentiment. Said Kubiak *"Good, I'm finally glad they made it. I'm sure everybody is happy when you consider the bad situation they had to go through last year in Seattle."* Kubiak goes on to say *"I spent six years in the minors and I wasn't looking forward to going through it all over again at that ballpark up there. It's certainly not up to Big League standards. Milwaukee has a great set up there and the people are major league."*

Lauzerique said he was grateful that it happened, *"Milwaukee is a major league town. It has a major league ballpark and a major league clubhouse. The people there are real good major league fans. Deep down I was hoping it would happen."* When asked about the players feelings during the days of uncertainty Lauzerique said *"It's been a guessing game for all the guys. They were just going crazy,"* he pointed out *"They had families with them and were looking for places to stay. They're all enthused."*

Manager Dave Bristol, tasked with the job of putting the players through their paces and getting the team ready for opening day said that *"The players are relieved that the decision was finally made. It's made it easier for them"* said Bristol. *"I was most concerned about them, because without players you're nothing. All I know is that I'm going to manage the best I know how and do everything I can to put a good club on the field."*

Enthusiasm ran citywide and as the news spread, Milwaukee mayor Henry Maier released a statement that read *"I've never felt that Milwaukee lost its Major League status. I think the Major Leagues lost Milwaukee and I think baseball is darn lucky to have people like the Brewers management standing in the wings to bail them out. I don't think I would have been that patient. 5 years is a long time, but the waiting is paid off."*

"So now let's back the new Brewers just as they were the world champions. If I know my Milwaukee it won't be long before the fans will have them right up there and in contention.

So welcome to the new Brewers and congratulations to the man who made the return of Major League Baseball to Milwaukee possible."

Plans were made for the players to fly to Milwaukee from Tempe, Arizona at the conclusion of spring training as the organization had seven days prepare Milwaukee County Stadium to host major league baseball for the 1970 season. With only a week to sell tickets for opening day the club decided that tickets for the April home schedule would be available only at the stadium box office and no mail order would be accepted. With tickets ranging from $1 for bleacher seats to $5 for mezzanine the Brewers' ticket prices were some of the best in baseball and the team was expecting a large turnout.

The task of getting Milwaukee County Stadium ready to host baseball was already underway before the final ruling awarding the team to Milwaukee came through. Although there was some sense of urgency having the ballpark ready in a week was not the Herculean task it may have seemed.

After all, it's not as though the stadium had been vacant since the departure of the Braves. The stadium had hosted twenty "home" games for the Chicago White Sox the past two seasons, in addition to being a home-away-from-home for the Green Bay Packers for several games each season. With Wisconsin's harsh winters making year-round maintenance of the playing surface next to impossible, especially considering the toll three NFL games a season took on the turf, the grounds crew was nonetheless confident that the ballpark would be ready come opening day.

Radio and television broadcast rights were quickly were awarded, with the radio rights going to WEMP-AM. Long-time Milwaukee baseball fans would remember WEMP as the radio home of the Braves until their departure after the 1965 season. Handling the radio assignments would be veteran broadcasters Merle Harmon and Tom Collins, both of whom handled the Braves broadcasts their last two years in Milwaukee. Harmon, who most recently called Minnesota Twins games on the radio and

Collins, the voice of Marquette Warriors basketball were familiar to Milwaukee baseball fans and brought instant credibility to the team's broadcasts. Fans could catch select Brewers road games on WTMJ TV channel 4, with Harmon and Collins joined in the booth by Dan O'Neill. WTMJ was also the former television home of the Milwaukee Braves but this time there would be a marked difference. For many years Braves owner Lou Perini fought to prevent Braves games from being televised because he thought attendance would suffer if fans could stay at home and watch the team. He finally relented in 1962 allowing fifteen Braves road games to be televised. This time around Milwaukee baseball fans would be able to see their newly-minted Brewers on TV much more often when they were away from home. In 1970 Milwaukee had two daily newspapers, the morning Milwaukee Sentinel and the afternoon Milwaukee Journal, and both papers gave ample coverage to the Brewers imminent arrival. Even though Lew Alcindor and the Milwaukee Bucks were in the midst of a deep NBA playoff run, coverage of the Brewers dominated not only the sports section but the front page also in the first days following the team being awarded to Milwaukee. There would be no lack of media coverage for the Brewers as they prepared for opening day.

While things were coming together relatively quickly for the Brewers there was one thing the quick turnaround time proved to be an insurmountable obstacle. That would be uniforms. Although the uniforms that the Pilots wore in Seattle were unique, they were not what Bud Selig had in mind. Selig wanted to outfit the Brewers in the red and blue colors of his childhood team, the minor league Milwaukee Brewers. Those Brewers had a rich baseball history in the city of Milwaukee and modeling the new Brewers uniforms after them would tap into that rich tradition. There doesn't seem to be any definitive information as to what those uniforms may have looked like. Several different variations appeared in newspaper articles, each showing a different style. An April 3rd UPI photo showed manager Dave Bristol wearing what appeared to be a home jersey with BREWERS across the front (in a font style very similar to the California Angels' uniforms) alongside catcher Jerry Mc Nertney, still outfitted in the Pilots' uniform. A different wire service photo showed a young woman modeling a pinstripe jersey with the Brewers name across the front in script, similar to what the team would later wear in the early 1990s. Pitcher Marty Pattin was also featured in a photo in the same style jersey worn by Bristol. Any one of these designs would have been an outstanding choice but it was all for not. Not only did the short turnaround time make this a difficult proposition at best, the fact that the players equipment was delayed coming from Arizona necessitated a quick solution to prepare for opening day. The team took the existing uniforms and removed the "Pilots" word mark from the front and replaced it with "Brewers" in block letters and went with a simple royal blue cap with a gold block letter M, almost identical to that worn by the Milwaukee Braves. Although initially it may have been considered a temporary solution, the team maintained the royal blue and gold color scheme well into the 1990s. Although the home uniform did not have the unique features that the Pilots displayed, the road uniform featured a mixture of capital and lowercase letters spelling out Brewers on the front of the jersey. Whether this was intentional or not it certainly was different.

It wasn't just the Brewers ball club that was affected by the short notice of the franchise transfer. The Topps Chewing Gum Company, longtime baseball card manufacturer, was left with a quandary. The springtime months mean young boys are gearing up to purchase the new season's baseball cards and 1970 was no different. Although there were rumors of the franchise shift for months, Topps had no choice but to go ahead and issue the early cards with the Pilots team name. It's understandable that initially the company couldn't take a chance that the sale wouldn't go through and opted to issue the first series with the Pilots designation. However, as was standard practice, Topps issued their baseball cards in individual series throughout the summer. The first series usually arrived in late March or early April to coincide with the beginning of the season, while the final series hit the stores in August. It's understandable that the first and probably the second series had already gone to press prior to the move being final; however the later series cards could have been adjusted to feature the new Milwaukee Brewers in place of the defunct Pilots. It's interesting that some of the cards featured pictures taken during spring training 1970 and appeared later in the spring and summer. And no doubt it likely caused some confusion when the young fans opened up a pack of baseball cards and wondered who these Pilots were and why they didn't exist in the standings anymore. Considering the troubled existence of the Seattle Pilots it was probably apropos that Topps gave the team a swan song appearance after they ceased to exist. Those Pilots cards from 1970 are somewhat popular with today's collectors as they are a reminder of a team and a time long gone. While the Brewers may have been left out of the major manufacturer's baseball card set they weren't entirely ignored. Flavor-est Milk issued a 24 card collector set featuring members of that first Brewer team. Original sets are very scarce today and the entire set has since been re-printed on several occasions. Ironically four years later in 1974, with rumors of an almost certain move of the San Diego Padres to Washington DC, Topps jumped the gun and featured a group of Padres player cards with the team listed as "Washington Nat'l League". Needless to say the Padres stayed in San Diego and the company scrambled to correct the error, creating a unique collector's item.

Meanwhile back in Tempe, the players were preparing to wrap up spring training and get ready to head north to Milwaukee for the 1970 season. The club would win their first game as the Brewers, defeating the Cleveland Indians 9-4 with slugging outfielder Danny Walton going four-for-four with a three-run homer, three singles, a walk and five runs batted in. Walton was shaping up to be one of the biggest surprises in spring camp and was looking like a future star in the making. There was also a reason to be optimistic with the Brewers prospects on the infield. Mc Nertney and Roof made a solid combo behind the plate, and the ever solid Mike Hegan at first base, lightning fast Tommy Harper at 2nd, Ted Kubiak at short and the veteran Rich Rollins at third base, gave the team the makings of a solid infield. While the outfield was still a question mark, the hard-hitting Walton looked to have played his way into a starting job. Like most teams, pitching would determine how far the team would go, and the Brewers were no exception. Starting pitchers Gene Brabender and Lew Krausse both had strong springs and looked to lead the Brewers rotation. The tragic loss of young prospect Miguel Fuentes in the off-season would be felt even more if some of the other young arms didn't step up.

As the club was trimming the roster to get down to the 25-man limit one of those pitchers that was being counted on just a year prior to stabilize the staff saw his time with the club come to an end. Left-hander Steve Barber was once one of the young up-and-coming pitchers in Major League Baseball.

Debuting in 1960 with the Baltimore Orioles Barber was a two-time All-Star and won 91 games his first seven years in the big leagues. Injuries derailed his career and he was never able to regain his All-Star status. After an injury-plagued 1969 season with the Pilots it was hoped that Barber would be healthy and ready to contribute in 1970, but was ultimately released on April 1st. Ironically Barber would resurface with the Brewers again in 1974 and once again he was released in spring training before the season began.

As spring training wrapped up the roster began to take shape although there were a few surprising cuts at the end of camp. Right handed relief specialist Dave Baldwin was sent down to Triple-A Portland, in spite of a good performance in spring training, and veteran utility infielder John Donaldson was also sent to Portland. The biggest roster surprise came on April 4th when the Brewers pulled off their first trade. The Brewers acquired third baseman Max Alvis and outfielder Russ Snyder from the Cleveland Indians in exchange for two promising young prospects, outfielder Roy Foster and infielder Frank Coggins. Both players would provide a veteran presence with Snyder providing extra insurance after the club placed outfielder Mike Hershberger on the 21 day disabled list. While both Alvis and Snyder would provide solid contributions, Foster would go on to club 23 home runs with the Indians while posting a solid .263 batting average. It would have been interesting to see what kind of one-two punch Foster and Walton could have provided in the middle of the Brewers lineup. The club also purchased outfielder Ted Savage for the Cincinnati Reds with the intention of platooning him and Snyder in the outfield. The team wrapped up their spring training schedule with an 11-3 loss to the Cleveland Indians before packing for Milwaukee. A reception was planned for the club when they arrived at the airport and the players and staff looking forward to finally meeting the fans in their new hometown.

CHAPTER SEVEN

Sunday April 5th 1970. The City of Milwaukee was preparing for the arrival of the Milwaukee Brewers from their spring training facility in Tempe Arizona. A reception was planned at General Mitchell Field to greet the team when their plane arrived. Local dignitaries were on hand to meet the team and fans were encouraged to gather in the concourse to show their support to their new hometown heroes. Fans started arriving as early as 7:30 p.m., two and a half hours before the team's scheduled arrival and by the time the Brewers' United Airlines flight touched down at gate five the crowd had swelled to almost 8,000. As the players and their families were escorted through the cheering throng, fans sang "Take Me Out to the Ballgame", many of them carrying colorful banners welcoming the team to Milwaukee. After a brief ceremony the players prepared for a motorcade to the Schroeder-Sheraton Hotel. Two buses took the players downtown while many fans followed behind honking their horns as a motorcade made its way to downtown Milwaukee. The players were amazed at the sight they saw when they arrived in Milwaukee. Pitcher Bob Meyer remembers "*The reaction of the city and fans was very positive and heartwarming. When we flew into Milwaukee from spring training there was a huge turnout at the airport and people were on the streets into town and on the way to the hotel. I think every player on the team was impressed and felt the love and attention that was showered on the team. I found the people of Milwaukee to be very welcoming and accepting. Milwaukee was starving for a team and they seemed to want a team and be involved with them.*" Several hundred fans were waiting at the hotel when the team arrived. Outfielder Danny Walton said "*I thought we would get a welcome, but never one like this!*" Jerry Mc Nertney's reaction was similar to Walton's, as he told a Milwaukee Sentinel reporter "*It's really great to be here. I'm really overwhelmed at the enthusiasm of the people. I didn't expect anything like this.*" While the players were making the trek from Arizona to Milwaukee activity at County Stadium continued at a brisk pace as a stadium workers were getting ready for the home opener. The concession stands were cleaned and stocked with supplies and beer on Sunday, with the food being delivered on Monday. All Milwaukee beers would be on sale at the opener and the concession stands would be ready to go by Tuesday. After checking the field on Sunday, American League officials certified the dimensions of the field for play. Stadium officials said the field would be playable but noted that more than a normal amount of damage had been done during the football season because of poor weather conditions. The turf on the field didn't knit as well as expected after the football season and some wetness remained in the outfield. There was no doubt though that the playing surface would be ready to go when the first pitch was thrown out.

A capacity crowd of 650 filled the Grand Ballroom over the Pfister Hotel on Monday April 6th for a "Welcome Brewers" luncheon sponsored by the Metropolitan Milwaukee Association of Commerce. As the band played "Happy Days Are

Here Again", "On Wisconsin" and "Take Me Out to the Ball Game", the crowd gave standing ovations to the Brewers board members and the team itself. By the time the Brewers convened at Milwaukee County Stadium for an afternoon workout 17,000 advance tickets had already been sold for opening day, with officials hoping for a crowd of upwards of 30,000. At that afternoon workout this is what the 25-man roster looked like:

Pitchers - Bob Bolin, Gene Brabender, John Gelnar, Lew Krausse, George Lauzerique, Bob Locker, Bob Meyer, John Morris, John O' Donoghue, Marty Pattin

Catchers- Jerry Mc Nertney, Phil Roof

Infielders- Greg Goossen, Tommy Harper, Mike Hegan, John Kennedy, Ted Kubiak, Rich Rollins, Max Alvis

Outfielders- Wayne Comer, Mike Hershberger, Steve Hovley, Ted Savage, Russ Snyder, Sandy Valdespino, Danny Walton

In less than 24 hours the City of Milwaukee would once again host their own Major League Baseball team. The city was ready, the stadium was ready, and the players were ready. If the weatherman cooperated the fans would fill the stands as the next generation of Milwaukee baseball began.

CHAPTER EIGHT

April 7th 1970. After four long years without baseball the city of Milwaukee was ready to welcome their new heroes, the Milwaukee Brewers, to County Stadium. Unlike 1953 when the Braves came to Milwaukee, there would be no Matthews, or Spahn or Logan on this team. This Brewers team was one year removed from an expansion club and there were no superstars or future Hall of Famers on this club. Nevertheless the fans didn't care, because baseball was back where it belonged.

The grounds crew and stadium staff had spent the prior six days getting the stadium ready to host Major League Baseball once again. As of the previous evening 17,500 advance sale tickets had been sold for Tuesday's opener, and club officials were hopeful that the inaugural game would draw 30,000, depending on cooperation from the weatherman. And cooperate he did as the first-pitch temperature was expected to be 55 degrees with partly sunny skies, perfect baseball weather for April in Milwaukee.

Their opponents, the California Angels, were coming off a strong spring training and were expecting big things in 1970. 24 year old right-hander Andy Messersmith, fresh off a 16 win season in 1969 was tabbed as the opening day starter. Messersmith, combined with lefty Clyde Wright, who to go on to win 22 games in 1970 and right-hander Tom Murphy, who pitched in with 16 wins, gave the team a formidable starting rotation. The Angels featured a strong lineup led by shortstop Jim Fregosi and left fielder Alex Johnson. Their infield was particularly strong with first baseman Jim Spencer and second baseman Sandy Alomar. Third Base was the only weak spot on the infield, which was remedied with a late April trade of opening day starter Aurelio Rodriguez and outfielder Rick Reichardt to the Washington Senators for slick-fielding power hitter Ken McMullen.

The Brewers would counter with right-hander Lew Krausse. Krausse made his major league debut at the age of 18 in 1961 with the Kansas City Athletics and posted a 2 and 5 record in 12 games with the Athletics. After spending the next two years in the minor leagues he would spend the next 6 years alternating between the starting rotation and the bullpen for the A's, first in Kansas City and later in Oakland. A January trade brought Krausse to Milwaukee along with Mike Hershberger, Phil Roof, and Ken Sanders in exchange for Don Mincher and Ron Clark. The Pilots/Brewers were active during the 1969-1970 off-season, completing transactions that would send 11 players from the 1969 Pilots elsewhere, while forming the roster for 1970. The transactions didn't end after spring training as trades on April 4th and April 5 brought Max Alvis and Russ Snyder from Cleveland and outfielder Ted Savage from Cincinnati, with Alvis and Snyder being in the opening day starting lineup and Savage appearing is a pinch hitter.

37,237 fans filed into Milwaukee County Stadium and created an electric atmosphere not seen since the Braves abandoned the Cream City in 1965. Sure there had been baseball since then, the Chicago White Sox played a handful of games in Milwaukee in 1968 and 1969, but that wasn't the same. The White Sox belonged to Chicago and they were just coming by for a visit. The Brewers belonged to Milwaukee, and it was like welcoming home a loved one after a long absence.

There were plenty of dignitaries to go around that day. Baseball commissioner Bowie Kuhn and American League President Joe Cronin were there to represent Major League Baseball. In a bit of bittersweet irony Fred Haney, the manager who led the Milwaukee Braves to the World Championship in 1957, was on hand as a special consultant to the Angels. Also on hand were Wisconsin Governor Knowles and Milwaukee Mayor Henry Maier. The players from both teams were introduced by Milwaukee sportscaster Earl Gillespie and the Brewers, their home white uniforms radiant in the

April sunshine, received a thunderous round of applause as Milwaukee showed their love to these new heroes. The pregame festivities wrapped up as County Executive John Doyne fired the first pitch to catcher Jerry Mc Nertney, and the moment that Milwaukee baseball fans had waited for was about to begin.

After Krausse's first pitch to leadoff hitter Sandy Alomar, play was halted as the ball was removed ready to be sent to Cooperstown to mark this historic occasion. Alomar would ground out to second base and the first out in Brewers history was in the books. Krausse was able to get consecutive flyball outs from Jim Fregosi and Bill Voss, and the Brewers first inning was 3 up and 3 down. Messersmith then matched Krausse, retiring the Brewers in order in the bottom of the first.

The second inning would not go as well as leadoff hitter Alex Johnson tripled to center field giving the Angels a runner in scoring position with no one out. The next batter, first baseman Jim

Spencer, flew out to deep centerfield driving in Johnson and the Angels took a 1-0 lead. Krausse was able to limit the damage and get out of the inning down by just one run.

The Brewers recorded the first hit in team history as right fielder Steve Hovley's one out single gave the Brewers their first base runner. Catcher Jerry Mc Nertney would fly out to center and third baseman Max Alvis would strikeout stranding Hovley with the Brewers still down by one.

After a three-run third inning by the Angels, Krausse's day would come to an end, being lifted for pinch hitter Rich Rollins in the bottom of the third. His replacement, John Gelnar would not fare much better giving up four runs, three of them earned, without recording an out, before being replaced by George Lauzerique, and by the bottom of the fourth the Brewers were down 8-0.

The rest of the afternoon would not go much better for the Brewers as they managed only a single from Tommy Harper and a single and double from

Steve Hovley. The Angels would go on to tack on four more runs against the Brewers bullpen, making the final score on opening day 12-0.

After the game manager Dave Bristol said *"The fans were great. They were just dying for something good to yell about. Maybe we tried too hard. I know that deep down our players want to do well. They have pride and they want to win. Tomorrow? Well, we'll show up"*.

Although the fans may have been disappointed by the final score, you wouldn't have noticed it as some of the fans throughout the game took the opportunity the show the entire stadium how happy they were to have baseball back. Occasionally a few young fans would jump on the field and run across with a banner, clearly against the rules but the attendants tried to be a little indulgent. 14 people, including 9 juveniles aged 13-17 were taken into custody however. By the middle of the ninth inning things started to get out of hand and there was a genuine free for all as fans streamed down to the field and about a dozen of them engaged in scuffles with the attendants until police arrived. The field was cleared though and the game was able to be completed without incident. While that type of behavior is unusual today and would be dealt with swiftly and severely, the world was a different place in 1970. There was no malice involved, just fans sharing their unbridled joy about baseball finally returning to their beloved hometown.

At the end of the day 37,000 plus fans were treated to their first taste of Major League Baseball after four barren seasons, and even though the Brewers came out on the short end of the score, the fans and the city were winners.

CHAPTER NINE

As the city of Milwaukee was still basking in the afterglow of the return of Major League Baseball the players were getting ready to play game 2 of 162 once again facing the California Angels. Although the team dropped the home opener, that day was more about the rebirth of baseball in Milwaukee than the tally on the scoreboard.

7,575 fans would show up on a relatively warm and windy afternoon in hopes of seeing the Brewers secure their first victory. Although the attendance seems like a huge drop off from Opening Day, this was not unusual for baseball in that era. Only the Dodgers, and surprisingly the Montreal Expos, drew more than 10,000 fans that day. Most teams drew in the five to six thousand range for weekday games, so the Brewers brass had to be happy with the turnout for game two.

The Angels would send right-hander Tom Murphy to the mound and the Brewers would counter with Marty Pattin. Both teams would field the same starting lineups with the Brewers hoping for a different result than Opening Day.

This time the Angels struck quickly as leadoff hitter Sandy Alomar ripped a double to left field. The next batter, third baseman Jim Fregosi grounded into a 1-3 put out sending Alomar to 3rd. Angels' right fielder Bill Voss singled to left field scoring Alomar, and after only three batters the Angels had a 1- 0 lead. Pattin would walk Alex Johnson before getting Jim Spencer to ground into a 3-6-1 double play, limiting the damage to just one run in the first inning.

Murphy would retire the Brewers in order in the bottom of the first and Pattin would counter, giving up a lone single to catcher Joe Azcue in the top of the second inning. The Brewers would only manage a two-out walk off of Murphy in the bottom of the inning, running their scoreless inning streak to

11. Pattin would give up a one-out single to Fregosi and right fielder Bill Voss collected his second RBI of the day as he doubled to left field scoring Fregosi giving the Angels a 2-0 advantage.

That would be it for the scoring as Pattin would settle down and pitch into the seventh inning with the Brewers only down by two runs. Leadoff hitter Ted Kubiak would line out to second base, and manager Dave Bristol, looking to get some offense going, sent up Sandy Valdespino to pinch-hit for Pattin. Valdespino struck out before Tommy Harper drew a two out walk. With Russ Snyder at bat, Harper stole second before Snyder doubled to right field scoring Harper, cutting the deficit to 2-1 and giving the Brewers their first run in franchise history. Greg Goossen would pinch-hit for first baseman Mike Hegan and draw a walk bringing up Danny Walton. A passed ball sent Snyder to third giving the Brewers runners on the corners, but Walton struckout looking ending the rally with the Brewers only down by one run.

That would be it for the Brewers' scoring for the day as the Angels scored two runs in the eighth and two more in the ninth inning bringing the final score to 6-1. Pattin had a strong outing going seven innings giving up only two runs seven hits, keeping the Brewers close going into the late innings. For the second day in the row the bullpen gave up multiple runs, and that was a sign of a problem that would plague the team for the early part of the season.

Although the fans may have been disappointed that the Brewers had yet to tally their first victory, that quick two game home stand showed that the people of Milwaukee with support their team win or lose. The team would next head down to Chicago the face the White Sox in search of their first victory.

Although the Brewers had dropped their first two games by a combined score of 16 to 1 the fans and the local media were still positive and supporting of the franchise. After all, the team was one year removed from being an expansion franchise and had a new manager along with quite a few new players still getting used to each other. The White Sox on the other hand were not only struggling on the field they were also struggling at the gate. After drawing a little over 11,000 on opening day, a cozy gathering of 1,474 showed up to White Sox Park watch the Sox drop a 6 to 4 decision to the Minnesota Twins. After the attendance figures for the Sox home away from home games in Milwaukee in 1969, the paltry showing for the first two games at home had to make the Sox ownership second guess their decision to remain in Chicago.

Things would not get any better on Friday afternoon as only 1,036 fans showed up at White Sox Park for their first glimpse at the Milwaukee Brewers. The fans that did show up saw the Brewers jump on starter Gerry Janeski right away in the first inning, as singles by Tommy Harper and Russ Snyder put runners on first and second with nobody out. Steve Hovley sacrificed the runners over and the next batter Danny Walton, singled to centerfield driving in both Snyder and Harper, giving the Brewers their first lead of the season.

Brewers' starter Gene Brabender would work a quick first inning retiring the White Sox in order, and then promptly led off of the top of the second with a double to left field. Brabender would be stranded as the next three batters went down in order with the Brewers still leading 2 - 0. The big right-hander ran into trouble immediately in the bottom of the second giving up a walk and a single before allowing a two-run double to Ken Berry. The White Sox would come back and score three more off of Brabender in the fifth inning before he was replaced by John Gelnar. Gelnar and John Morris combined to throw 3 and 2/3 innings of scoreless ball keeping the Brewers in the game, as the Crew added one run in the eighth on a double by Tommy Harper that scored Ted Kubiak. On the same play Rich Rollins was thrown out on a bang-bang play at the plate, leaving the score at 5-3. The Brewers would add one more in the top of the ninth, but it wasn't enough as they dropped a 5-4 decision to the White Sox.

Although thus far the news on the field wasn't great, off the field it was good news all around. Earlier in the day the team announced that they had sold more than 3,800 season tickets thus far, an astounding number considering the short period of time that tickets had been on sale. They also announced that they resolved several scheduling conflicts with the Green Bay Packers regarding the use of County Stadium. The Brewers game against the Indians at August 15th was moved to June 2nd as part of a Twilight double header, and the Brewers game against the White Sox on September 5th would be switched to July 9th. The Packers had preseason games scheduled with the Chicago Bears on August 15th and the Cincinnati Bengals on September 5th, no doubt scheduled long before the team moved to Milwaukee.

The team would be 0-3 heading into Saturday afternoon's game against the Sox, looking for their first win of the season with Bob Bolin tabbed to face White Sox left-hander Billy Wynne.

CHAPTER TEN

The Brewers were winless entering Saturday afternoon's game against the White Sox. With a game time temperature of 39 degrees only 2,600 die-hard fans showed up at White Sox Park continuing the White Sox run of sparse attendance. The Brewers would send right-hander Bob Bolin to the mound facing the White Sox' Billy Wynne, with the team in search of their first victory.

Bristol went with the same lineup from Friday's game hoping to generate some offense against the White Sox staff. The White Sox would strike first in the bottom of the first as future Hall of Famer Luis Aparicio homered off of Bolin giving the White Sox a 1 - 0 lead. In the bottom of the third Bolin would issue a walk to Walt Williams who promptly stole second base. Aparicio singled to left sending Williams to third, as Aparicio would steal second. Carlos May would triple scoring Aparicio and Williams giving the White Sox a 3 - 0 lead. Third baseman Bill Melton would pop up to short for the first out of the inning. Catcher Duane Josephson drove in May with a sacrifice fly to right field before Bolin would strikeout Tommy McCraw to end the inning. By the end of the third the Brewers were down 4 - 0.

In the meantime Wynne was cruising along allowing only two hits through five innings, a two-out single to Hovley in the first and a one-out double to Walton in the fourth who was thrown out trying to stretch it into a triple. Wynne opened the sixth inning giving up a leadoff double to Russ Snyder before getting Hovley to ground out to short. The red-hot Danny Walton then crushed a Wynne offering for a two-run home run cutting the White Sox lead in half. A bit of history was made as Walton's blast was the first home run in Brewers history, and no doubt energized the Brewers dugout.

Bob Meyer and John O'Donoghue would come out of the pen and hold the White Sox scoreless through the 7th. In the top of the 8th

Wynne would retire the first two batters before giving up a two-out single to center to Steve Hovley. That brought Danny Walton the plate, and once again Walton would hammer another 2-run home run, tying the game at 4.

O'Donoghue would retire the White Sox 1-2-3 in the bottom of the 8th setting up the Brewers for some ninth-inning heroics. Max Alvis would reach on a single to centerfield and the next batter, Ted Kubiak, would reach on an error on the pitcher. Rich Rollins singled to left field sending Kubiak to 2nd and scoring Alvis. Tommy Harper struck out for first out of the inning. Russ Snyder singled to right scoring Kubiak and sending Rollins to second. The next batter, Steve Hovley continued his hot start by doubling to center scoring Snyder and Rollins and putting the Brewers up 8 - 4. Walton and Mc Nertney would both ground out ending the inning, leaving the Brewers three outs away from their first victory.

Bristol went with veteran Bob Locker in the bottom of the ninth and the righty quickly dispatched of the White Sox in order. Gail Hopkins lined out to shortstop Ted Kubiak securing the Brewers first win in franchise history, an exciting 8 - 4 come-from-behind victory.

There were plenty of heroes to go around on this day. The bullpen was outstanding, pitching five innings of one-hit baseball, giving the Brewers the opportunity to claw their way back into the game. Center fielder Steve Hovley continued his torrid start going 3 - 5 with two RBIs and two runs scored. But the real hitting star of the day was without a doubt Danny Walton. The big slugger went 3 - 5 with a pair of two-run homers, upping his season average to .444. As a team the Brewers pounded out 13 hits and came back from a 4 - 0 deficit, scoring all eight of their runs in the last four innings. The comeback victory had to be satisfying for a team that struggled to score in its first three games. With the hot bats at the top of the order and the outstanding work from the bullpen that first victory gave the fans reason for optimism.

The Brewers and White Sox wrapped up their first series of the season with a Sunday double header on a chilly afternoon in Chicago. Opening Day starter Lew Krausse was set to square off against White Sox lefty Tommy John in the first game of the twin bill.

An error by White Sox third baseman Bill Melton allowed leadoff batter Tommy Harper to reach base in the top of the first for the Brewers. The lightning-fast Harper would steal second base with center fielder Steve Hovley at the plate. Hovley would sacrifice Harper over to third and the Brewers would have a runner in scoring position with one out for catcher Jerry Mc Nertney. John would induce Mc Nertney into a 6-3 ground out with Harper scoring, giving the Brewers a 1-0 advantage. Danny Walton would follow up with a single to right but first baseman Greg Goossen struck out ending the Brewers half of the first.

Krausse would issue a walk to shortstop Luis Aparicio and a single to Bill Melton but he was able to get catcher Duane Josephson to pop out to first base ending the threat and leaving the Brewers with a 1-0 advantage after one inning. The Brewers would jump on John immediately in the top of the second inning as third baseman Max Alvis singled to right field, and Ted Kubiak followed up with a single to right advancing Alvis. After a groundout by Snyder, Krausse ripped a single to right field scoring Alvis and moving Kubiak to third base. John would get Harper to fly out to right field, but then uncorked a wild pitch to the next batter, Steve Hovley, allowing Kubiak to score from third. Hovley would ground out to second to end the inning but the Brewers tacked on two more runs and had a 3-0 lead over the White Sox after an inning and a half.

Both pitchers settled down with John retiring the Brewers in order in the top of the third and top of the fourth, while the White Sox went three up and three down against Krausse in the bottom of the third. The Sox would touch Krausse for a run in the bottom of the fourth as leadoff hitter Carlos May doubled to right field and third baseman Bill Melton would fly out to center. Catcher Duane Josephson singled to left field scoring May making the score 3-1. The next batter, Tommy McCraw reached on a fielder's choice and center fielder Ken Berry would follow up with a walk, but Krausse would escape trouble again as he got second baseman Bobby Knoop to ground out ending the inning.

Both teams would be retired in order in the fifth inning with the Brewers maintaining a 3-1 lead. Mc Nertney led off the top of the sixth with a single to center field, and Danny Walton would crush his third home run in the past two days giving the Brewers a 5-1 lead. Chicago would counter in the bottom of the sixth as lead-off hitter Carlos May homered off of Krausse cutting the lead to 5 - 2. Krausse walked Josephson and McCraw before being replaced by John Gelnar. Gelnar would get center fielder Ken Berry to ground into a double play ending the inning with the score 5-2 Milwaukee.

Gelnar would pitch 3 and 2/3 innings of scoreless relief, scattering four hits and shutting out the White Sox the rest of the way and the Brewers would have their second win in a row and a chance to even their record the win in the nightcap of the doubleheader.

In game two the Brewers would send right-hander George Lauzerique to the mound, facing White Sox lefty Gerry Arrigo. The Brewers went down in order in the top of the first while the White Sox led off the bottom of the first with single by Syd O'Brien. Aparicio would ground into a 6-4-3 double play and Carlos May grounded out to first with the game scoreless after one inning.

The Brewers would send 10 men to the plate in the top of the second inning, with walks to both Walton and Goossen bringing Max Alvis to the plate. Alvis would double to left scoring Walton, and catcher Phil Roof drew a walk loading the bases. Centerfielder Russ Snyder would walk, forcing in another run, pushing the Brewers lead to 2-0. Lauzerique would help his own cause by lining a single the left scoring Alvis, leaving the bases still loaded and nobody out. Ted Kubiak then singled to left scoring Snyder. Hovley would ground into a fielder's choice and Kubiak would be thrown out stealing at third base, ending the inning, with the Brewers plating five runs, all charged to the starter Arrigo.

Lauzerique continued to roll retiring the White Sox in order in the second and only giving up a single to Ken Berry in the third inning, while White Sox reliever Tommy Sisk retired the Brewers in order in the top of the third. The Brewers would strike quickly in the top of the fourth as Roof and Snyder both singled and Lauzerique reached on an error to load the bases. Tommy Harper would strikeout looking for the first out of the inning. Kubiak would reach on an error on the second baseman and Roof scored leaving the bases still loaded with only one out. Hovley doubled to center scoring Snyder and Lauzerique, while the next batter, Danny Walton would fly to deep center field scoring Kubiak for the fourth run of the inning. Greg Goossen would strike out to end the inning and the Brewers would hold a commanding 9 - 0 lead.

Lauzerique made short order the Sox in the fourth only surrendering a one-out single to Carlos May. The Brewers jumped on Sox reliever Tommy Sisk again in the fifth inning as Max Alvis led off with a single and Phil Roof reached first on a fielder's choice. Snyder reached on the second error of the day on second baseman Syd O'Brien bringing up the pitcher. Lauzerique would launch a three-run homer off of Tommy Sisk, giving the Brewers a 12-0 lead. Kennedy and Kubiak singled on back-to-back at-bats, and center fielder Steve Hovley greeted new White Sox pitcher Gene Rounsaville with a single to left scoring Kubiak. Danny Walton grounded into a double play bringing the inning to an end as the Brewers tacked on five more runs and had a commanding 13 - 0 lead.

Lauzerique cruised through the fifth and sixth innings, allowing only a single to Ken Berry before slugging third baseman Bill Melton touched him for a solo home run with nobody out of the seventh. That would be all the scoring for the Sox in the inning and both teams were retired in order in the eighth.

The Brewers would strike again in the ninth as Snyder would reach on a one out walk, and Kennedy reached on an infield single. Kubiak drew a walk loading the bases, and Hovley singled to right scoring Kennedy and Snyder, advancing Kubiak to third. Hot hitting Danny Walton singled to left driving in Kubiak before Greg Goossen popped out to first, ending the inning with the Brewers up 16-1.

Lauzerique walked the first batter in the bottom of the ninth before getting two quick outs. A single by Gail Hopkins put runners on first and second and Buddy Bradford singled to center scoring Hopkins. Lauzerique struck out Walt Williams looking and the Brewers wrapped up the sweep with a 16-2 pasting of the Pale Hose in Chicago.

The Brewers now had a three-game winning streak and evened their record at 3-3. The club received solid contributions up and down the lineup and the star of the weekend had to be pitcher George Lauzerique. The right-hander threw a complete game and limited the White Sox to two runs while going two-for-four with a home run and four RBIs. Outfielders Danny Walton and Steve Hovley continued their hot hitting while the bullpen came up big in the first two games of the series. There was definitely reason for optimism amongst Brewer fans as the club stood at .500 after the first week of the season.

CHAPTER ELEVEN

The Brewers were a confident bunch as the team sat at 3 - 3 when they departed for a two-game series with the Oakland Athletics. The pitching was solid, with both the starters and the bullpen rounding into form. After a slow start the offense came to life and put up some impressive numbers, led by the scorching hot tandem of Danny Walton and Steve Hovley. Manager Dave Bristol told the Milwaukee Sentinel *"Danny started looking good the last 10 or 12 days of spring training, and won himself a job. He had a good spring and I hope he can keep it up."* Bristol added, *"Our trade with Cleveland for Alvis and Snyder is paying off. This team scored 19 runs twice during spring training and I knew it explode soon."*

The news off the field we just as encouraging as advance ticket sales continued at a brisk pace, no doubt encouraged by the Brewers' recent showing. Without the offseason to sell tickets the club would be at a decided disadvantage compared to the rest of the league, but sales continued as the fan base showed its increasing interest in the new team. Hoping to win back some old admirers and attract some new ones, the club announced they were sponsoring their first Ladies Day of the season on Thursday April 16th at County Stadium when the Kansas City Royals came to town for a quick one game showdown. General manager Marvin Milkes said that ladies attending Thursday's game will be admitted for $1. He also added that Ladies Day tickets would not be sold in advance. In addition to the bargain admission price the ladies will be given a 12 page brochure entitled "Baseball for Dolls", and will be treated to a playing field seminar on baseball strategy and rules featuring manager Dave Bristol and several Brewers players. In this day and age a promotion such as Ladies Day would be considered quaint by some, but it was a very common and popular promotion throughout Major League Baseball dating back to the 1940s. Bill Veeck, considered by some to be the father of ballpark promotions, was known for sponsoring Ladies Days at Borchardt Field when he owned the minor league

Milwaukee Brewers. Promotions such as this would begin to wane throughout the 1970's but, in some ways they are reminder of more innocent times.

When it came to promotions in 1970, Oakland Athletics owner Charles O. Finley was in a league by himself. Dating back to his days as owner of the Kansas City Athletics Finley was without peer when it came to promoting his team. Whether it was dressing his players in brightly colored uniforms complete with white shoes, trotting out a mule as a team mascot, or donning a Beatles wig and offering the lads from Liverpool a then-record $150,000 for a one-night performance in Kansas City, the man known as Charlie O always had a trick up his sleeve. Another thing Finley could do was assemble a talented ball club, and the team that the Brewers would face already had the core of players who would in a few years become known as the "Swingin' A's", capturing three straight World Series titles.

The Brewers rolled into Oakland to face the A's for their home opener and A's owner Charlie

Finley requested and amazingly received permission to use gold colored bases for the A's home opener. What effect the brightly colored bases had on the game is unknown but, the Brewers dropped a 2-1 heartbreaker, managing only three hits off of Oakland starter Jim "Catfish" Hunter. Things were not as close the following evening as the A's hitters roughed up three Brewers pitchers in a 9-1 Oakland victory before a cozy gathering of 2,900.

While the Brewers were heading home after their brief two-game series in Oakland, a potential tragedy was developing. An explosion in the service module on the Apollo 13 space capsule put the crew in peril as their disabled craft was more than 200,000 miles from Earth. Mission Control in Houston worked feverishly to come up with a plan to bring the astronauts safely back to Earth, while the world watched as these events unfolded.

Back home on Earth the Brewers made news on an off-day when general manager Milkes announced that he had invited the Atlanta Braves to play an exhibition game against the Brewers on Thursday May 14th. Milkes said *"A game between the Brewers and Braves can't help but be a tremendous attraction for fans throughout Wisconsin."* The May 14th date was suggested because neither team had a league game and both will be in the area. The Braves play in Chicago on May 12th and will be idle until opening a series in Cincinnati on May 15th. Although only a handful of players that were with the Braves while they were in Milwaukee were still on the roster, Milwaukee baseball fans would still welcome the opportunity to see the Braves one more time.

On Thursday morning April 16th Milwaukee woke to the news that the Apollo 13 astronauts had made a successful correction which would send them on a course for Earth, with a scheduled splashdown for Friday afternoon. Americans across the country breathed a sigh of relief as the Apollo astronauts averted a tragedy and would be able to bring their crippled spacecraft back home.

7,100 fans showed up at County Stadium on a 64-degree afternoon to watch the Kansas City Royals take an 8-6 decision from the Brewers. The Royals jumped out to a quick two run lead in the first inning, then tacked on six more runs by the fourth inning and the Brewers were down 8 - 2. Starter Lew Krausse was touched for six runs on six hits in just three innings pitched, but only four of those runs were earned as the defense let the pitching staff down by committing three errors on the day. The Brewers losing streak stood at 3 games as the Chicago White Sox made their first appearance in Milwaukee since 1969, this time as a visiting team.

The Apollo 13 astronauts were safely home by the time the Sox pulled into Milwaukee for their three-game series. The Pale Hose were looking to avenge the drubbing they took in Chicago at the hands of the Brewers a week prior and took the first step as the Brewers blew a 5-2 lead, allowing the Sox to stage at 8 - 5 come-from-behind victory. Starter Bob Bolin and relief pitcher John Gelnar give up a total of 8 runs before righty Bob Locker could stem the bleeding as the White Sox rapped out 17 hits while the Brewers shaky defense committed two more errors which ultimately proved to be the Brewers undoing. The Sox would have to wait though if they wanted to fully avenge their losses as Milwaukee's springtime weather washed out a Sunday afternoon doubleheader. At 1 p.m. when the first game was scheduled to start the temperature was 38 degrees, with winds gusting up to 25 miles an hour, yet more than 6,000 fans were already in the stands and officials said over 10,000 tickets had been sold for the game. After a steady rain continued during the delay the decision was made to cancel both games as the team was scheduled to fly to Anaheim for a three game series starting on Monday. The Brewers would then head east to Boston, Washington, and New York wrapping up a road trip that would consist of 14 games in 13 days.

The warm California weather did nothing to cure the Brewers' ills as the club dropped its 5th straight, a 10 inning heartbreaker to the Angels 5-4. The Brewers carried a 3 - 0 lead into the bottom of the 7th before the Angels scored four runs on five hits to take a 4-3 lead. The club would tie the game in the top of the 8th on an RBI single by Danny Walton and the score would remain tied until the bottom of the 10th when Roger Repoz drove in Alex Johnson giving the Angels a ten inning walk-off victory. Things wouldn't get any better as the Brewers power outage continued, only managing three hits off of Angel starter Tom Murphy dropping at 3 - 1 decision for their six consecutive defeat. Off the field rumors were swirling that the Brewers were interested in Angels' outfielder Rick Reichardt. Reichardt, a former University of Wisconsin athlete from Stevens Point was one of baseball's first bonus babies and still considered to have a large upside. After hitting .254 with 13 home runs and 68 RBIs for the Angels in 1969, Reichardt had spent most of the 1970 season as a bench player and occasional pinch-hitter. Angels' general manager Dick Walsh said *"I understand the Milwaukee club is interested in Reichardt too, but I haven't talked with Marvin Milkes about him. We'll talk trade, but we have to have a proven player, somebody like Tommy Harper, Jerry Mc Nertney, Bob Bolin, or Gene Brabender perhaps."* The Brewers were noncommittal when asked about any potential deal, but Reichardt's raw ability had to be intriguing to the Brewers front office. Considering the club's continuing offensive woes the rumors surrounding the outfielder's possible deal to Milwaukee could not be ignored. The team closed out the first leg of the road trip with another 3-1 loss to the Angels. Angel lefty Clyde Wright held the Brewers to one run on six hits while going the distance handing the club their seventh straight loss. Prior to the game the Brewers activated Mike Hershberger from the disabled list, optioning Sandy Valdespino to AAA Portland. Hershberger had been nursing a strained groin since spring training and the club was hoping his presence would inject some additional offense into the lineup.

With the Brewers record sitting at 3 − 10, the club set off to Boston for a three-game set against the Red Sox. While the starting pitching had for the most part kept them in most of their games, the bullpen had no margin for error with the offense struggling as much as it was. Bristol had tried several different combinations and had yet to find a lineup that could produce on a nightly basis. Both the club and their fans were hoping that the team's fortunes would turn around on the East Coast swing of the road trip.

Not willing to wait for the Brewers fortunes to turn around a woman identified as Witch Barbara, claiming to be an authentic witch, entertained a gathering of more than 1,000 people at a County Stadium event promoted by radio station WOKY, to cast a friendly spell on Milwaukee's new baseball team. Beginning at 4:30 am, Witch Barbara stood with radio station personality Bob Barry in a black circle of cloth, around which four candles burned, and lead the costumed crowd in a chant. Whether or not a bit of witchcraft would help the Brewers, you have to give kudos to the crowd for showing up that early in the morning to support the team in their own unique fashion!

The Brewers' hopes of ending their seven-game losing streak would have to wait an additional day as the series opener against the Red Sox was washed out and rescheduled as part of a Saturday doubleheader. The Brewers sent Lew Krausse to the mound in game one while the Red Sox countered with right-hander Sonny Siebert. Milwaukee scored first, plating one run in the top of the first inning as Tommy Harper scored on a wild pitch, but when the Red Sox answered with three in the bottom of the inning on a Rico Petrocelli home run it was beginning to look like the losing streak would continue. The Brewers responded with three runs in the second and six more in the top of the third making the score 10 − 4, while Krausse and reliever Bob Locker shut the Red Sox down the rest of the way giving the Brewers their first victory in their last eight games. Second baseman Tommy Harper continued his hot hitting going four for five, scoring three runs, driving in two and stealing two bases while raising his average above .300. Things did not go as well in game two as the Brewers dropped a 3-0 decision, only managing four hits against Red Sox lefty Gary Peters. Brewers starter Bob Bolin didn't pitch that badly, giving up three runs on four hits, but once again the Brewers offense could not put together any scoring opportunities. The club did bounce back in the series finale scoring a 5-3 victory on the power of 8 and 2/3 strong innings from starter Gene Brabender. The Brewers took a 5-1 lead into the ninth inning and were able to hold off a Boston rally as Bob Locker shut the door, registering his third save the season. The team picked up their second series win of the season and took a 5-11 record into DC for a four-game series versus the Senators.

In a bit of irony and timing, any hopes the Brewers had of landing Angels outfielder Rick Reichardt ended when the outfielder was dealt to Washington earlier in the day. While the Senators received Reichardt and third baseman Aurelio Rodriguez from the Angels the cost was high as the Nats sent third baseman Ken McMullen to the Angels. McMullen was one of the best glovemen in the game in addition to being able to hit for power, making it unlikely that the Brewers could have put together a package that would have been acceptable to pry Reichardt away from the Angels. If the Brewers were going to boost their offense, help would have to come from elsewhere.

In the series opener against the Senators the Brewers found themselves down 3-0 after four innings as Marty Pattin struggled again giving up three runs and five hits. The Brewers would come back to score two in the fourth on Tommy Harper's first home run of the season to deep left field. John Morris, John Gelnar, and Bob Meyer came in and held the Senators scoreless the rest of the way and the Brewers tied the game on Danny Walton's leadoff home run to start the ninth. The Brewers would strike again in the top of the tenth. Third baseman John Kennedy led off with a single to right field and moved to second on a sacrifice bunt by Tommy Harper. Ted Savage would follow with a double to left field scoring Kennedy staking the Brewers to a 4-3 lead. After a walk to Hovley and a strikeout to Danny Walton, Savage and Hovley executed a double steal putting runners at second and third. Senators' reliever Horacio Pina would intentionally walk Mike Hegan to load the bases. Pina uncorked a wild pitch scoring Savage and advancing the runners before finally getting out of the inning.

De-facto closer Bob Locker would come in to face the Senators in the bottom of the 10th and immediately walked Rick Reichardt and issued a single to John Roseboro. Pinch-hitter Jim French drew a walk loading the bases for Ed Brinkman. Brinkman lined a single to right scoring Reichardt and Roseboro tying the game before Locker was replaced by John O'Donoghue. Center fielder Ed Stroud laid down a sacrifice bunt but O'Donoghue's throw to first went wild allowing French to score as the Brewers lost a 6-5 heartbreaker in 10 innings. Unfortunately that is as close as the Brewers would get the rest of the series as the Senators swept all four games, closing it out with a 12-2 drubbing of the Brewers to end the month of April.

The Brewers ended their first month with a dismal record of 5 - 15, eight games behind the Western Division leading Minnesota Twins. It should be noted that the Brewers played 16 out of those first 20 games on the road and it was hoped that some home cooking would be just the tonic they would need to string together some wins. Not that there were no bright spots, outfielders Danny Walton and Steve Hovley were both hot the entire month with Walton providing a power bat from the cleanup spot. The weak link that first month of the season was the pitching staff, and the bullpen in particular as manager Dave Bristol and pitching coach Wes Stock were still trying to find the right combinations. The month of May would find the weather warming up, in addition to a 13 game home stand, as the Brewers looked for a spark to provide their new found fans with winning baseball.

CHAPTER TWELVE

The month of May did not start any better as the Brewers dropped a 6 -3 decision to the New York Yankees. The lone bright spot was once again Danny Walton. The scorching hot leftfielder crushed a monster 440 foot home run into the left field bleachers, tying him for the AL home run lead with Washington's Frank Howard. Once again the starting pitching was roughed up early, putting the Brewers in a 4 -0 hole after four innings. The next day wasn't much better as starting pitcher Marty Pattin was only able to last 1/3 of an inning, giving up 4 runs on five hits before being replaced by John Morris. Yankee lefty Fritz Peterson held the Brewers in check through 5, surrendering only an infield single to John Morris.

The Brewers finally got to Peterson in the sixth as John Kennedy led off the inning with a sharp single to center and Tommy Harper followed a Rollins strikeout with a walk. Ted Kubiak stroked a single to center scoring Kennedy and moving Harper to second. Peterson would strike out Savage for the second out before walking Danny Walton to load the bases. Rightfielder Mike Hershberger looped a Peterson offering into center scoring Harper and Kubiak, cutting the Yankee lead to 4 -3. Lindy Mc Daniel replaced Peterson and got pinch hitter Mike Hegan to strike out looking to end the inning.

John O'Donoghue and John Gelnar combined to set the Yankees down in order in the sixth and seventh innings while the Brewers went quietly in the seventh. Tommy Harper led off the eighth inning with a strikeout but the next batter, Ted Kubiak singled to right field. Kubiak moved to second on a wild pitch by Lindy McDaniel and took third on a single by Ted Savage. Yankee manager Ralph Houk summoned righty Jack Aker from the bullpen to face Walton. "Dangerous Danny" didn't disappoint as he ripped an Aker offering to left field, scoring Kubiak and moving Savage the third tying the score at 4. Catcher Thurman Munson was called for obstruction on the ensuing run down play allowing Savage to score from third putting the Brewers up by one. Aker retired Hershberger and Hegan on ground outs to end the inning with the Brewers ahead 5-4. Gelnar continued mowing down the Yankees, retiring them in order in the bottom of the eighth.

Catcher Jerry Mc Nertney led off the top of the ninth for the Brewers, crushing a Joe Verbanic pitch to deep left field giving the Brewers a 6-4 lead. John Kennedy would walk, with Gelnar reaching on a fielder's choice. Tommy Harper walked and Ted Kubiak singled to left loading the bases for the Brewers with just one out. Once again Houk went to the Yankee pen bringing in lefty Steve Hamilton, and Hamilton went on to strikeout Savage and Walton to end the inning.

Bristol stuck with Gelnar for a third inning of work, even though there were fresh arms in the bullpen. The wheels quickly fell off as Gelnar gave up a leadoff single to Jerry Kenney followed by a game-tying home run by Bobby Murcer to deep right field. The next batter, Roy White doubled to right field and Bristol went to his bullpen bringing in Bobby Bolin, probably three batters too late. Bolin struck out first baseman Danny Cater and issued an intentional walk to Jim Lyttle looking to set up the double play. It was all for naught as catcher Thurman Munson singled to right, scoring White and giving the Yankees and come-from-behind 7- 6 victory.

Once again it was late inning pitching that proved to be the weakest spot on the Brewers' roster, although the starting pitching had been spotty for the early part of the season to begin with, there was no margin for error for this staff. That was evident the following day as the Brewers jumped out to a 5-0 lead against the Yankees before blowing leads of 6-2 and 7-5 and finally falling to the Yankees 8-7 in game one of a Sunday doubleheader.

Lew Krausse came up strong in game two, pitching a gem for six innings giving up only one run, before being touched for three runs in the bottom of the seventh. The Brewers briefly held a 2-1 lead but were unable to score any more against journeyman John Cumberland and relief specialist Lindy McDaniel. The loss ran the Brewers losing streak to eight games as they prepared to head back to Milwaukee for the first extended homestand, a 14 gamer starting the following Tuesday against the Red Sox. The club hoped some home cooking and familiar surroundings would pull the team out of their early-season funk and put some wins on the board for the Brew Crew.

After an off-day on Monday, the Brewers returned to Milwaukee County Stadium to start a three-game series with the Boston Red Sox. 6,700 fans showed up on a chilly and windy Tuesday evening the welcome to Brewers home, hoping to see the hometown nine string together some victories. Starting pitcher Gene Brabender not only dazzled the fans but the Red Sox hitters as well, as he was spinning a gem, throwing a perfect game through 5 and 2/3 innings. Unfortunately things went bad quickly as the Red Sox hitters battered the big right-hander, scoring five runs on 3 hits, leaving the Brewers in a 5-0 hole. The Brewers were only able to muster three hits off of Red Sox starter Sonny Siebert as they dropped their ninth straight game 6 - 0.

Prior to Wednesday's game the Brewers released third baseman Rich Rollins and recalled right-hander Skip Lockwood from Triple-A Portland. The Brewers hoped that Rollins could provide veteran leadership at third base, but Rollins' .200 batting average and the emergence Tommy Harper at third base made him expendable. The 23 year old Lockwood was sporting a 4-1 record in five starts with a nifty 2.65 ERA. The Brewers coaching staff looked for Lockwood to slide into the starting rotation and hopefully provide some stability as the season moved forward. General Manager Marvin Milkes had intimated during the last road trip that changes would be coming and this move would be a harbinger of more to come.

The Brewers would finally register their first win at County Stadium with a 4 - 3 decision over the Red Sox. Powered by a solo home run from Ted Kubiak and a three-run blast from second baseman John Kennedy, along with a strong performance from Bob Bolin the 5,300 fans that showed up on Wednesday evening went home happy. Bolin went eight strong innings giving up three runs on five hits while striking out 10, and John Gelnar came in and shut the door in the ninth for his second save of the season. The Brewers starting rotation was having a rocky time to start the season and Bolin's strong outing came at the perfect time to give the bullpen a rest.

Another strong outing from the starting rotation, this time from Lew Krausse, propelled the Brewers to a 5-1 victory over the Red Sox before a crowd of 8,194 on a warm spring evening. With a game-time temperature of 79 degrees Krausse was hot from the beginning scattering five base hits through 7 2/3 innings. Slugger Danny Walton powered his ninth home run of the season in the seventh inning, and outfielder Russ Snyder chipped in with the other two runs and that was all the offense the Brewers would need on this evening. John Gelnar would come in and pitch the last 1 1/3 innings to pick up his third save of the season and second in his many nights.

On the field the Brewers now had a two game winning streak and were ready to welcome the Washington Senators into County Stadium for a three-game series. Just a week earlier the Senators had swept four from the Brewers and the club would be looking to even the score. Off the field, Major League Baseball released the 1970 All-Star ballot and surprisingly the only Brewer on the ballot was third baseman Tommy Harper. While Harper was a strong candidate, a case could be definitely made for Danny Walton and even Steve Hovley as both we're having strong years to date. The fans would be voting once again for this year's All-Star Game in Cincinnati and both Hovley and Walton were strong write-in candidates.

CHAPTER THIRTEEN

The Brewers opened a three-game series against the Ted Williams led Washington Senators on a warm overcast afternoon at County Stadium. The visiting Senators would send Kenosha native Joe Coleman to the mound while the Brewers would counter with John Morris, making his first start of the 1970 season. The Senators would have a strong Wisconsin connection in this game as in addition to Coleman, Green Bay native Frank Howard, and Stevens Point native and one time Brewers' trade target Rick Reichardt would be in the lineup.

Morris retired Washington three up and three down in the top of the first inning, while in the bottom of the first only Harper reached on a throwing error by Senators' second baseman Dave Nelson. The Senators could only manage a one-out single by Hank Allen before Ed Stroud grounded into a double play to end the inning. The Brewers struck first in the bottom of the second as a Steve

Hovley ground out was followed by consecutive singles from Kubiak and Mc Nertney. Second baseman John Kennedy laid down a bunt that was fielded by Bosman who went to first, allowing Kubiak to score putting the Brewers up 1 - 0.

Morris set the Senators down in order again in the top of the third and the lefty was looking sharp in his first start of the season. Tommy Harper led off the bottom of the third off with a walk but was caught stealing with Mike Hegan at the plate. Hegan drew a one-out walk from Bosman and the next batter, Russ Snyder singled to left moving Hegan to third base giving the Brewers runners in scoring position with just one out. Danny Walton rifled a single to left field scoring Hegan and putting the Brewers up 2-0.

Morris continued to mow down the Senators giving up only a hit batsman and a single through six innings. In the meantime, the Brewers were not able to muster any offense themselves, only registering a sixth inning single off of Bosman. Reichardt led off the top of the seventh for the Senators with a ringing double to right field bringing up third baseman Aurelio Rodriguez. Rodriguez crushed a John Morris offering deep to left field that the Brewers thought had gone over the fence and bounced back. Reichardt scored while Rodriguez pulled into third base with a triple. That brought Senators' manager Ted Williams out of the dugout to protest to the umpires that it was a home run. The umpires ruled correctly that the ball did not clear the fence and Rodriguez stayed at third, where he was subsequently caught in a rundown on Ed Stroud's grounder for the second out of the inning. Stroud would score on Paul Casanova's single to center, tying the game at two, before Morris would retire Bosman to end the inning.

The Brewers could only muster a one-out double from Jerry Mc Nertney in the bottom of the seventh before pinch-hitter Wayne Comer flew out to left to end the inning. Once again Dave Bristol went to John Gelnar out of the bullpen and he was able to work around a hit by pitch and intentional walk to retire the Senators in the 8th. Tommy Harper led off the bottom of the 8th with a 6 - 3 ground out. Mike Hegan singled and the next batter, Russ Snyder doubled to left, moving Hegan to third. Williams went to lefty Darold Knowles out of his bullpen and he issued an intentional walk to Danny Walton to load the bases. Williams played the lefty-righty percentages again bringing in right-hander Horacio Pina to face the right handed hitting Ted Savage. Savage would fly out to right field and the next batter, Ted Kubiak, would ground back to the pitcher to end the inning, leaving the bases loaded in the score tied at two. Both Gelnar and Pina retired the opposing batters 1-2-3 in the ninth inning sending the game into extra innings. Gelnar would give up a one-out single to Mike Epstein in the top of the tenth before getting Brinkman and Allen to ground out keeping the game tied at 2.

Williams went to his bullpen again bringing in Joe Grzenda. Grzenda struck out Tommy Harper looking to begin the top of the 10th. First baseman Mike Hegan singled to right field putting the game-winning run on base for the Brewers. Bristol went to his bench, bringing in the right handed hitting Mike Hershberger to face the lefty. Hershberger would fly out to right field for the second out of the inning. Grzenda then hit Danny Walton with a pitch, putting runners on first and second with two outs. Williams summoned starter Joe Coleman from the bullpen an attempt to snuff out the Brewer rally. Ted Savage would work Coleman for a two-out walk, loading the bases for Ted Kubiak. With two outs in the inning, Kubiak laced a Coleman offering to center field scoring Hegan, and giving the Brewers a dramatic ten inning, 3 - 2 walk off victory.

Needless to say the 8,900 fans that showed up for that Saturday afternoon game can say they saw the most exciting game at County Stadium so far that season. The Brewers got an outstanding outing from John Morris and another clutch relief performance from John Gelnar to run their winning streak to three games. Maybe the warm weather and some home cooking was just what the doctor ordered to get the Brew Crew on the winning track.

The Brewers would ride a three game winning streak into a Sunday afternoon doubleheader against the Senators. On a beautiful 72° afternoon, a crowd of 13,941 came out hoping to see the win streak extended.

The Brewers would send Gene Brabender to the mound to face Senators' lefty George Brunet. Brabender worked a 1-2-3 first inning while in the bottom of the inning Ted Savage doubled to left scoring Ted Kubiak giving the Brewers a quick 1 - 0 lead. Brabender set the Senators down in order in the second while the Brewers managed just a leadoff single by Greg Goossen in the bottom of the second. Brabender ran into trouble in the third inning as he gave up a leadoff double the Bernie Allen and a walk to Jim French. Brunet laid down a sacrifice bunt moving the runners-up and Ed Brinkman singled to left scoring Allen and French giving the Senators a 2-1 lead. Brabender retired Ed Stroud on a ground out and struck out Frank Howard the end the inning with the Brewers down by one run.

Neither team could generate much offense until the bottom of the fifth inning. John Kennedy led off with a single to left field but was erased on a fielder's choice grounder by Brabender. Hoping to catch the Senators off guard Brabender took off for second base and would have been caught stealing but, the big right-hander slid hard into second base kicking the ball out of Bernie Allen's glove. Tommy Harper popped-up to first base and the next batter, Ted Kubiak tripled to center scoring Brabender, tying the game at two. Ted Savage followed with a triple to center scoring Kubiak and the next batter, Danny Walton singled to left scoring Savage making the score 4 - 2. That ended Brunet's day as Ted Williams brought in Dick Such to get the final out of the inning.

The Brewers gave one of those runs back in the top of the six as Brabender gave up a leadoff double to Stroud who moved to third on a sacrifice by Frank Howard. First baseman Mike Epstein flew out to center field scoring Stroud and making the score 4-3. In the bottom of the sixth, Bristol sent

Mike Hegan up to pinch-hit for Brabender ending his day on the mound with the big right-hander in line for the win. The Brewers came up scoreless in the bottom of the sixth as John O'Donoghue took the mound for the Brewers to start the seventh inning. O'Donoghue retired Hank Allen on a fly ball to right but then gave up a one-out single to Dave Nelson. Rick Reichardt came to the plate and promptly launched a two-run home run to deep left-centerfield putting the Senators in front 5-4. O'Donoghue would walk the next two batters before finally striking out Mike Epstein to retire the side.

Horacio Pina took the mound for the Senators and retired the Brewers 1-2-3 in the bottom of the inning keeping the score at 5-4. O'Donoghue got the first out in the top of the eighth and was replaced by George Laurzerique who retired the final two Senators batters to end the inning. A bottom of the eighth leadoff single by pinch-hitter Russ Snyder and a single to center by John Kennedy gave the Brewers runners on the corners with one out. Williams went to left-hander Darold Knowles who struck out Mike Hegan and induced a 6 - 3 ground out from Tommy Harper to end the Brewers' threat in the bottom of the eighth.

Bristol brought in Marty Pattin to pitch the ninth, and the righty retired the Senators in order sending the Brewers to the bottom of the ninth down by one. The deficit didn't last long as Ted Kubiak launched a solo home run to left field tying the game at five. Knowles walked Ted Savage and give up a double to Danny Walton putting runners on second and third with nobody out. Knowles would intentionally walk Jerry Mc Nertney loading the bases with the pitcher's spot coming up. Bristol went to his bench once again sending up the right-handed-hitting Wayne Comer to pinch-hit for Pattin. Comer was 0 - 17 on the year but, he was the only bat left on the bench besides backup catcher Phil Roof. Comer would come through as he lashed a single to left field scoring Ted Savage and giving the Brewers another exciting walk off victory and the team their fourth straight victory.

The fans in the stands would barely have time to catch their breath as the Brewers prepared for game two, sending the newly-promoted Skip Lockwood to the mound for his first start. Lockwood would navigate a first-inning walk turning it over to the Brewers offense in the bottom of the inning. Leadoff hitter Tommy Harper doubled to centerfield and moved to third on a sacrifice by Russ Snyder. A walk to Mike Hegan put runners on the corners for Danny Walton. The big slugger would strike out, but the next batter Steve Hovley singled to left field scoring Harper. Second baseman Ted Kubiak would follow up with his own single the left field scoring Hegan making the score to 2-1. Lockwood would continue to pitch efficiently and effectively, only surrendering a single to John Roseboro in the top of the third. In the Brewers half of the third Mike Hegan would launch a home run to deep left field scoring Russ Snyder making the score 4-0. Lockwood would set the Senators down in order in the fourth and in the bottom of the inning Tommy Harper homered to deep left field making a score 5 -

0 in favor of the Brewers. Lockwood would continue his mastery of the Senators surrendering a walk and two singles through six innings. In the bottom of the sixth Kennedy would lead off the inning with a groundout and Lockwood would help his own cause by cracking his first major league home run to deep left field giving the Brewers a 6-0 lead. Lockwood would give up two singles in the seventh, going into the eighth inning with a 6-0 lead. In the top of the eighth Lockwood would strike out big Frank Howard but the following batter, first baseman Mike Epstein homered to deep centerfield putting the Senators on the board. Lockwood would give up a single to right field to Lee Maye, and an RBI double to Aurelio Rodriguez. Bristol would go to his bullpen once again bringing in Marty Pattin and Lockwood's day was done. The right-hander had an outstanding debut for the Brewers, pitching 7 1/3 innings giving up three runs, only one of them was earned, while striking out five. Pattin would get the first batter he faced, Bernie Allen to pop out to third for the second out of the inning. Paul Casanova would reach

on an error by third baseman Tommy Harper allowing Rodriguez to score making it is 6-3 ball game. Rick Reichardt would hit his second homer in as many days off of Pattin, scoring Casanova making it a 6-5 game before Pattin was able to retire Ed Brinkman for the third out of the inning.

The Brewers were only able to manage a one-out walk in the bottom of the eighth and headed into the ninth inning with a 6-5 lead. Pattin would strike out the first batter Hank Allen but the next hitter, Frank Howard crushed a home run to deep centerfield tying the game at six. John O'Donoghue would come in from the bullpen and retire the last two batters ending the inning with the score tied at six. Joe Grzenda took the mound for the Senators in the bottom of the ninth and Ted Savage promptly greeted him with a single to center field. A Mike Hegan strikeout would bring Danny Walton to the plate. Grzenda would a uncork wild pitch sending Savage to second base before walking Walton to put runners on first and second. Williams would bring Horacio Pina in from the bullpen to face the hero of game one Wayne Comer. Comer reached base on a fielder's choice and Pina issued an intentional walk to Ted Kubiak looking to set up the double play. Jerry Mc Nertney would pinch hit for Phil Roof and line a single to right field scoring Savage and giving the Brewers their third consecutive one-run walk-off victory. The crowd of almost 14,000 was delirious after watching their Brewers sweep a doubleheader in such exciting fashion. The Brewers had won five out of six on the home stand with the Yankees coming to town for a three-game series on Monday.

Off the field, the Brewers made a minor trade sending game one hero Wayne Comer to the Washington Senators in exchange for outfielder Hank Allen and minor league second baseman Ron Theobald. With the acquisitions of Savage and Snyder to begin the season, and the hot starts of Danny Walton and Steve Hovley, Comer was not seeing much time and was considered expendable. Although Allen was primarily an outfielder he could also play second, third, and first base, giving the Brewers additional versatility off the bench. This would prove to be just the first of many transactions to come for the club as the 1970 season wore on.

CHAPTER FOURTEEN

The Brewers welcomed the New York Yankees to town for the start of a three-game series with hopes of extending their winning streak. These were not the same Yankees that dominated the 1940s and 50s. Perhaps their biggest star, Mickey Mantle retired prior to the 1969 season, and pitcher Mel Stottlemyre was the only holdover from their last pennant-winning team from 1964. The Yankees thus far were hovering around the .500 mark and were still a few years away from pennant contention.

A crowd of a little over 4,800 turned out on a cold blustery Monday evening, and with a game-time temperature of 42 degrees and the threat of rain, the Brewers hoped to be able to get the game in before the rains came. The Brewers jumped out to a 3-0 lead in the bottom of the third thanks to some shoddy fielding by the Yankees. Starting pitcher Bob Bolin had so far held the Yankees in check. Bolin gave back one of those runs in the fourth then settled down and held the Yankees scoreless through seven. Bolin would help his own cause when he homered to deep left field in the bottom of the seventh giving the Brewers a 4-1 advantage. The Yankees picked up a run in the top of the eighth off of reliever Bob Locker and Milwaukee got that run back in the bottom of the eighth when Danny Walton singled to center scoring Russ Snyder.

The Brewers took a 5-2 lead into the bottom of the ninth inning, three outs away from their sixth consecutive win. Locker gave up a single to pinch-hitter Frank Tepedino, who was erased on a fielder's choice by Horace Clarke. Jerry Kenney reached on an infield single putting two on and Dave Bristol went to his bullpen, bringing a John O'Donoghue. Consecutive errors by John Kennedy and Tommy Harper allowed the Yankees to tack on two additional runs, ending O'Donoghue's night. George Lauzerique came in and got Danny Cater to ground out to third base as Bobby Murcer scored the tying run erasing the Brewers three-run lead. With the rain already starting the Brewers came up in the bottom of the ninth inning and a two-out single by Hank Allen followed by a two-out double by Tommy Harper put the winning run on third base, but Yankee reliever Ron Klimkowski got Ted Savage to ground out to third ending the inning. After a rain delay the umpires called the action, ending the game in a 5 -5 tie.

The rain threat lingered as the Brewers took the field the next day for game two, sending Lew Krausse to the mound against the Yankees Fritz Peterson. Once again the Brewers defense would let them down as Krausse would give up six runs over 4 2/3 innings, with only two of them earned. Two errors by Ted Kubiak, and one by a first baseman Mike Hegan contributed to the Brewers being down 8-0 after six innings. The Brewers would stage a rally in the bottom of the eighth scoring four runs on back to back home runs by Phil Roof, and Max Alvis, along with an RBI double from Mike Hegan. In the ninth, the Brewers exploded again, but the rally was cut short by a downpour that stopped the game.

With two outs and runners on first and third, Danny Walton, who had struck out four straight times previously, hit a towering fly into short center that fell between three Yankees for a double. The ball was caught by a gust of wind in the sudden thunderstorm allowing Tommy Harper to score Milwaukee's fifth run and put runners on second and third. But for a second straight night the umpires stopped the game because of rain, ending the Brewers winning streak at five games.

The Brewers wrapped up the series, sending John Morris to the mound against the Yankees and Morris pitched a gem, giving up only one run and three hits while striking out seven. Morris had shut out the Yankees for 8 2/3 innings before giving up a home run to Roy White. A three run home run by Ted Savage was all the offense the Brewers would need in a 3-1 victory, giving the Brewers a record of 6-2-1 on the home stand with four left to play.

Perhaps the most anticipated game of the home stand was one that wouldn't even count in the standings. On that Thursday the Brewers played an exhibition game against the Atlanta Braves. This would mark the Braves first appearance in Milwaukee since they abandoned the Cream City after the 1965 season. A crowd of 25,899 turned out in 40 degree temperatures with light rain falling to welcome back the Braves. The crowd gave Hank Aaron a standing ovation when he was introduced at a pregame ceremony. *"It certainly was the greatest thrill of my life"* said Aaron. *"The response was tremendous. I didn't expect that."* Three Braves that were with the team while they were in Milwaukee were in the lineup. Besides Aaron, the Milwaukee fans remembered - and cheered - left fielder Rico Carty and first baseman Tommie Aaron, Hank's brother. Signs welcomed past heroes like Aaron and Carty, and present heroes like Danny Walton, the Brewers hard-hitting left fielder.

"It feels nice to be back but the weather, is too cold." Carty said. *"It was a thrilling moment for me when I walked out on that field again,"* said Hank Aaron. *"I saw a lot of my old friends and fans out there in the right-field bleachers.*

You have to be a real baseball fan to come out on a night like tonight," the slugger said. *"This just proves that Milwaukee doesn't have to take a backseat to anybody as far as putting people in the stands."*

The fans also cheered for the Brewers and pitcher Skip Lockwood who shut out the Braves on six hits, and drove in the game's only run. On this night the good guys, the ones wearing royal blue and gold, prevailed as the Brewers drew the biggest crowd of the season since opening day. For one night at least, the wounds of that long contentious divorce back in 1965 were healed, and all was right in Milwaukee's baseball world.

When play resumed on Saturday the Twins showed why they were one of the favorites to appear in the Fall Classic as they defeated the Brewers in a slugfest, 11-7. Even though the Brewers hit three home runs in the game and rapped out 14 hits, the pitching staff gave up four home runs to the Twins and five Brewer pitchers issued 10 walks. On Sunday the Brewer bats fell silent before a crowd of

16,393 on a sunny afternoon in Milwaukee. The Brewers could only manage one run off of Twins starter Jim Perry and dropped a 6-1 decision. Brewers' starter Lew Krausse gave up five runs on eight hits over 5 2/3 innings and saw his record fall to three wins and seven losses. Krausse was a victim of the Brewers porous defense, as three of those five runs were unearned due to a pair of errors by John Kennedy, and one by Max Alvis. With the struggles that the pitching staff was having the Brewers needed better glove work keep them in the game. So discouraged was manager Bristol over the Brewers' lack of offense, he sent the team back out after the game for additional batting practice for the second day in a row. It was still early enough in the season to right the ship and Bristol was willing to do what it would take to get the Brewers on a winning track.

The Brewers had an off-day on Monday, and although things were quiet on the field the front office was busy. The Brewers obtained infielder Roberto Pena from the Oakland A's in exchange for minor leaguer John Donaldson. Brewers' manager

Dave Bristol said *"He can play every position in the infield, and he can swing a bat with some power. He has a chance to get some home runs here."* The acquisition of Pena put the Brewers one over the 25-man player limit. A Brewers spokesman said *"There might be another trade in the works"*, hinting at more moves to come. The acquisition of Pena may have been in response to the Brewers shoddy defense early in the season. Pena was solid with the glove and hopefully would plug a hole on the infield.

Prior to Tuesday's game the Brewers made two roster moves, sending Greg Goossen and John Kennedy to Portland and recalling infielder Gus Gil. The struggling Oakland Athletics came to town and sent right-hander Catfish Hunter to the mound while the Brewers countered with John Morris. The A's scored first when Felipe Alou drove in Bert Campaneris with a sacrifice in the top of the first inning. The Brewers would jump on Hunter in the bottom of the third, plating five runs on five hits, including an RBI single by the newly-acquired Roberto Pena. The newly-promoted Gil followed

Pena with an RBI single of his own driving in Hovley to wrap up the scoring in the inning. Morris would cruise the rest of the way giving up only a two-run home run to Reggie Jackson in the top of the sixth. Tommy Harper would homer in the bottom of the seventh to wrap up the scoring as Morris went the distance, scattering three runs on seven hits as the Brewers snagged a 6-3 victory.

The Brewers wrapped up their 14-day home stand on Wednesday night against Oakland. The A's jumped on starter Skip Lockwood in the first inning, scoring three runs while the Brewers countered with two of their own in the bottom of the first. The Brewers tied the game in the bottom of the fourth and took a lead in the fifth on a run-scoring single by Steve Hovley. The A's came right back and tied the game on a leadoff home run by Don Mincher in the top of the sixth, while the Brewers took the lead back on a two-out home run by Tommy Harper. The A;s would tie it up in the top of the seventh on a run-scoring single by Sal Bando and in the bottom of the seventh Russ Snyder would double home Hovley and Walton, giving the Brewers a 7-5 lead. The game would continue to seesaw back and forth as Oakland plated two in the top of the 8th as Rick Monday and Felipe Alou each drove in a run to tie the game again at 7. Reliever Marty Pattin held the A's scoreless in the top of the ninth, and Oakland manager John McNamara went to Rollie Fingers in the bottom of the inning. Fingers was able to get Jerry Mc Nertney to ground out before giving up a single to Steve Hovley. The next batter, Hank Allen, doubled scoring Hovley and giving the Brewers a walk off 8 - 7 victory before a crowd of 8,747.

The Brewers finished their first extended home stand of the season with eight wins and four losses, while playing some exciting baseball along the way. The club would go out on a quick six game road trip to Kansas City and Minnesota, before they would be back in Milwaukee for an 11 game home stand to wrap up the month of May and start out the early portion of June. No doubt the team was encouraged by their performance at home and hopes were amongst not only the players, but the fans too, that the Brewers could continue their progress and keep playing an exciting brand of baseball.

CHAPTER FIFTEEN

After an off-day on Thursday the Brewers began their next road trip in Kansas City against the Royals. Starter Bob Bolin looked sharp through three innings, giving up only two singles, while the Brewers jumped to a 2 - 0 lead against Royal starter Dick Drago. The Royals would get one of those runs back in the bottom of the fourth and would break the game open in the bottom of the fifth off of reliever Marty Pattin, scoring four runs off of Pattin to take a 6-2 lead .

Drago would hold the Brewers scoreless for the next three before giving way to Al Fitzmorris. Russ Snyder would drive in Savage for the Brewers last run of the game and they were shut down the rest of the way, losing game one of the series 6 - 3.

The Brewers met the Royals for a Saturday night tilt at Kansas City Municipal Stadium, and once again jumped out to a quick lead as they touched

Royals' starter Jim Rooker for one run in the top of the first. The lefty Rooker shut the Brewers down the rest of the way, scattering seven more hits while Brewers' starter Lew Krausse went 6 2/3 innings giving up three runs, with only two of them earned, as the Brewers dropped their second straight on the trip, by a 3-1 decision.

A Sunday afternoon crowd of 30,000 filed into Kansas City's Municipal Stadium on an 81 degree Sunday afternoon to watch the Royals and Brewers wrap up their three-game series. Kansas City jumped out to a quick three to nothing lead, scoring three in the bottom of the first off of John Morris, but the Brewers battled back and tied it up in the ninth inning at four. In the top of the tenth, Tommy Harper tripled off of Royals' reliever Moe Drabowsky, and Ted Kubiak raked a single to right field, scoring Harper giving the Brewers a 5 - 4 lead. Manager Bristol sent Gene Brabender out for a second inning of relief work and after retiring Ed Kirkpatrick on a groundout, gave up a single and two walks to load the bases. Bristol went to John

O'Donoghue out of the bullpen, and O'Donoghue gave up a single to center to former Milwaukee Brave Hawk Taylor, plating the winning run for the Royals and securing the sweep of the series.

The Brewers moved on to Minnesota to take on the division-leading Twins and once again their defense let them down. The Brewers took a 4-3 lead into the bottom of the seventh inning when three errors allowed three Twins runners to score, turning that lead into a 6-4 deficit. Skip Lockwood pitched well, scattering seven hits over eight innings giving up only two earned runs, but the Brewers porous defense resulted in four unearned runs, extending the Brewers losing streak with a 6-5 defeat. The streak continued the next day as the Brewers were only able to scratch out two runs on six hits off of emergency starter Jim Kaat. There were some bright spots, as Danny Walton appeared to be breaking out of the mini-slump he was in and Tommy Harper raised his average to .300 while socking his sixth home run of the season. The Brewers were going to need both of these big bats in the lineup if they were going to play competitive ball with five months still left in the season.

The weather gods took mercy on the Brewers washing out Wednesday's game and the club wrapped up the series with an 11-2 shellacking at the hands of the Twins. Although the Brewers rapped out eleven hits, they were only able to score two runs off Twins starter Luis Tiant, both on home runs by Russ Snyder and Tommy Harper. The Twins meanwhile battered five Milwaukee pitchers for eleven runs on sixteen hits. The Brewers limped home after losing all six games on the brief two city road trip finding themselves with a 13-29 record at the quarter point of the season, 16 and 1/2 games behind the division leaders. An 11-game home stand awaited them with manager Bristol still looking for answers for the team's woes.

Once again the Brewers would get close but did not have enough offense to overtake the Detroit Tigers, losing 5-4. Tiger lefty Mickey Lolich held Brewers to one run through seven innings, before being touched for three runs in the bottom of the eighth. Reliever Dennis Saunders would come in and shut the door as the Brewers dropped their seventh straight. Once again Skip Lockwood pitched well, but not well enough to earn the win, this time pitching on just three days rest. Lockwood would have one more start the next week before leaving for military service. Manager Bristol said *"Skip has faced some big bats since he was called up. He's pitched against Washington, the Atlanta Braves, Oakland, Minnesota and Detroit. He's got youth, a good arm and poise. And he's learning all the time."*

Bristol was also impressed with reliever Dave Baldwin who had been called up earlier in the day. Baldwin worked the final two innings giving up one hit, walking three, one intentionally, and striking out two. *"He got them out,"* Bristol said *"and that's what I like. They didn't score."* In addition to Baldwin's strong outing, Tommy Harper extended his hitting streak to 13 games giving the Brewers a potent force at the top of the order.

The Brewers would make another move prior to Saturday's game, recalling pitcher Ken Sanders from AAA Portland. Sanders was dazzling thus far in Portland posting a 4 - 1 record with an ERA of 1.06 in 34 innings of work. Sanders would give the Brewers another strong arm out of the pen and provide Bristol another late inning option.

The bats came alive Saturday night as the Brewers scored five runs in the bottom of the first, four of them on an inside the park grand slam home run by Roberto Pena. The game turned into a slugfest and the Brewers found themselves down 7 - 6 in the bottom of the eighth inning. RBI's from Danny Walton and Mike Hegan gave the Brewers the lead and they would hang on for a 9 - 7 victory.

A frightening moment occurred in the bottom of the first inning when Tiger outfielder Al Kaline collided with teammate Jim Northrup while they were chasing Pena's fly ball. Kaline was down, had swallowed his tongue and was in distress. Brewers' bullpen coach Jackie Moore and Kaline's Tiger teammate Willie Horton were credited with possibly saving Kaline's life. *"I could hear him gasping for air,"* Moore said *"and he was turning blue. I realized he had swallowed his tongue and tried to pry his jaws open. But the best I could do was just get two fingers between his teeth."* Horton raced over from left field and forced open Kaline's mouth. Curt Rayer, Milwaukee's trainer, then pulled Kaline's tongue from down his throat Moore said. *"I don't remember us hitting,"* Kaline said. *"I sort of remember Willie leaning over me and getting my mouth open."* *"I used a technique I learned when I used to box,"* Horton said. *"You put pressure on the nerves on the back of the jaw and that makes the man relax enough to let you pry his mouth open."* Kaline was taken to a local hospital where he spent Saturday night complaining of soreness in his lower jaw in the leg. He would be released and be in uniform the next day but would not see action for the club.

The Brewers would stage another thrilling come-from-behind victory on Sunday. The Brewers were down 5-2 going into the bottom of the eighth inning before scoring three on a double by Steve

Hovley, and a single from Danny Walton. Bristol went to Dave Baldwin out of the bullpen and he set the Tigers down in order setting up the Brewers for some ninth-inning heroics. Mike Hegan led off with a double to right field and was sacrificed to third by Ted Kubiak. After a walk to Hank Allen, Ted Savage scorched a double to left field scoring Allen and Hegan giving the Brewers a 7-6 come-from-behind victory. Baldwin picked up his first win of the season as the Brewers took two out of three from the Tigers. The Brewers would be off Monday before opening up a four-game home stand against the Cleveland Indians to start the month of June.

The Brewers finished the month of May with a record of 15-30 and were showing improvement. The bullpen seemed to be stabilized with the additions of Baldwin, and Sanders, and with the June trading deadline coming up it was likely there would be more moves made to strengthen the roster. With the weather warming up the crowds were getting larger which had to please Selig and the ownership group. Two months into the season the fans showed that they would support their new team and the players were giving 100% every game to show the fans how much they were appreciated. The Brewers may not have been pennant contenders yet, but they were taken into the hearts of Milwaukee baseball fans.

CHAPTER SIXTEEN

After an off day on Monday the Brewers returned to action on Tuesday with a twilight doubleheader against the Cleveland Indians. Originally scheduled as a single game, game two was tacked on as the original August 15th contest against the Indians conflicted with a preseason date the Packers had scheduled with the Chicago Bears at County Stadium.

The Indians sent hard throwing lefty "Sudden" Sam McDowell to the mound in game one and the fireballer tossed a masterpiece, holding the Brewers hitless through seven innings giving up only one run on two hits while striking out eight as the Indians took game one 4-1. In game two, Brewers' starter Skip Lockwood was rocked for seven runs on nine hits as the Brewers dropped a 9-5 decision before a crowd of 7,812 on a cool Tuesday night. One bright spot for the Brewers was the continued production of Danny Walton. Walton socked his

11th home run of the season and kept his average at the .300 mark, while anchoring the cleanup spot for the Brewers. Tuesday night's crowd brought the club's season attendance to 201,721 after 20 games. Considering the lousy weather during the first two months of the season, those numbers were more than respectable and were further evidence that the fans would come out to support the Brewers.

Once again starting pitching put the Brewers in an early hole as starter Lew Krausse only lasted one and 2/3 innings giving up four runs as the Brewers ultimately dropped a seesaw battle 7-6. Offensively the Brewers could put runs on the board but defense and starting pitching was still their Achilles heel.

The Brewers closed out the series with an 8-4 loss to the Indians. Earlier in the day the Brewers recalled 24 year old right hander Ray Peters to make his first Major League start. Peters only lasted two innings giving up four runs on six hits before giving way to the bullpen. The losing streak stood at four games as the defending American League champion Baltimore Orioles would be in town for a three game series Friday, Saturday, and Sunday.

Earlier in the day the Brewers would participate in their first June amateur draft. Holding the number four overall pick, the Brewers selected catcher Darrell Porter out of Southeast High School in Oklahoma City. Porter was tabbed as the best catching prospect to come out of the Southwest since Johnny Bench and it was hoped that the left-handed hitting backstop would move quickly through the organization. Porter would in fact see action the following year with the Brewers, making the jump from single A to the Major Leagues. After a cup of coffee in 1972 Porter would stick for good in 1973. Although Porter never lived up to the hype of being the next Johnny Bench, he was a solid backstop for the Brewers until he was traded to the Kansas City Royals after the 1976 season. In Kansas City, and later with the St. Louis Cardinals, Porter hit his stride as a solid catcher with power who handled the bat well. In a stroke of irony Porter would be named the World Series MVP as his 1982 Cardinals defeated the Milwaukee Brewers four games to three.

Second round pick Ken Pape did not sign with the club, opting to attend college at the University of Texas. The remainder of the draft for the Brewers produced career minor leaguers or players that never even went that far, with the exception of their number six pick left-handed pitcher Bill Travers. Travers was just 17 years old when selected by the Brewers and he was seen to have a high upside. Travers would work quickly through the Brewers minor league system debuting with the team in 1974 and was a fixture in the rotation for the next six seasons. Travers made the American League All Star team in 1976 and experienced the best success of his career as a member of manager George Bamberger's rotation from 1978 through 1980. Unfortunately, injuries sidetracked Travers career after signing a lucrative free agent contract with the California Angels in 1981, and after only making 14 appearances over the next three seasons his career was over.

The Brewers were also monitoring the progress of last year's number one pick power hitting Gorman Thomas. Thomas showed promise in 1969 playing rookie ball at Billings, and although he was struggling a bit at Class A ball he showed the power that the Brewers were hoping would develop. Originally drafted as an infielder Thomas was proving to be an error machine as he was tried at both shortstop and third base, and a position change was in order if he was going to continue to move up through the organization.

The first place Orioles came to town and a crowd of 13,548 saw a well-pitched game by both Oriole starter Dave McNally and Brewers' righty Bob Bolin. Bolin went the distance giving up three runs on six hits but McNally one of the Orioles' "Four Aces" baffled the Brewers allowing only two runs as Baltimore took game one of the series.

The Brewers put a stop to their losing streak in game two as leadoff hitter Tommy Harper continued to swing a scorching bat, reaching base a total of four times and increasing his league lead in stolen bases to 23. Danny Walton crushed a two - run home run in the fifth inning to put the Brewers up 6-2, while Ken Sanders and John Gelnar came in and shut the door securing a 6-4 win for the Brewers.

A crowd of almost 17,000 turned out on a beautiful 80 degree Sunday afternoon in Milwaukee for the rubber game of the series. The Brewers jumped out to a quick 2-0 lead which held up until the fourth inning. Baltimore scored two in the fourth, one in the fifth, and four in the top of the eighth to take 7-2 lead over the Brewers. In the bottom of the eighth the Brewers finally got to Orioles' starter Mike Cuellar, as singles by Allen and Hershberger put runners on the corners. Roberto Pena singled to drive in Allen, moving Hershberger to third base bringing up the pitcher's spot. Phil Roof pinch hit for Ken Sanders and blasted a Cuellar offering deep into the left field seats for a three-run home run bringing, the Brewers within one. The Brewers were able to get two on with one out in the bottom of the ninth, but Orioles' reliever Eddie Watt was able to retire McNertney and Hershberger ending the Brewers comeback effort.

Off the field the Brewers suspended outfielder Steve Hovley after he refused to pay a fine. *"I was fined for reporting 20 minutes late,"* Hovley said *"I was late for Thursday's game because I overslept."* The outfielder said he *"was not intentionally absent. It didn't seem logical to be fined. It's not the money, just the principle."* General manager Marvin Milkes confirmed that Hovley had been suspended and was being offered up for trade. The Brewers did have depth in the outfield, but Hovley was a talented young player and the Brewers could use all the bats they could get.

The Brewers would use a scheduled day off on Monday as a makeup date for an early season rainout against the Chicago White Sox. Leadoff hitter Tammy Harper would deposit White Sox starter Bart Johnson's first offering over the left field fence giving the Brewers a quick 1-0 lead. Lew Krausse went the distance for the Brewers, scattering six hits and two runs to record his fourth win of the season. Harper was heating up over the past several weeks and was giving the Brewers a potent force at the top of the order. The Brewers outfield of Walton, Savage, and Snyder were all hitting over .275 giving the Brewers a strong one through four in the batting order.

The Brewers would head out on an 11-game road trip to Detroit, Cleveland, and Baltimore wrapping up the trip with three in California versus the Angels. With the trade deadline coming up in a few days the Brewers were expected to be dealing as they tried to continue adding pieces to the roster.

The Brewers opened the road trip against the Tigers by taking a quick 2-0 lead on a two-run single by Danny Walton. Brewers' starter Ray Peters would not record an out as he gave up a single and two walks to the first three batters he faced, loading the bases for the Tigers. Skip Lockwood came out of the bullpen to replace Peters and struck out Norm Cash, but the next batter, Tigers slugger Willie Horton launched a Grand Slam home run to deep left field giving the Tigers a 4-2 lead. Horton would hit two more home runs in the game giving him three for the day as the Tigers routed the Brewers 8-3.

In game two of the series the Brewers would send Bob Bolin against Tigers' righty Earl Wilson. The Brewers held a 4-3 lead until the bottom of the seventh when the Tigers scored three runs off of relief pitcher John Gelnar on a two-run home run by Al Kaline, and a two-run single by pinch hitter Gates Brown. Mike Hegan would hit a leadoff home run to deep right field in the top of the eighth bringing the Brewers within two, but relief pitcher Tom Timmermann would shut the Brewers down the rest of the way giving the Tigers a 7-5 victory. After the game, rumors were rampant that the Brewers were close to a deal for suspended outfielder Steve Hovley, with Baltimore and Oakland being rumored as possible destinations. Relief pitcher Bob Locker and several other players were also mentioned in trade rumors as the Brewers continued to tinker with their roster.

The Brewers would pull the trigger on Thursday, shipping Hovley to the Oakland A's in exchange for left-handed pitcher Al Downing and infielder/outfielder Tito Francona. The 29-year-old Downing came up with the New York Yankees in 1961 and moved into the starting rotation in 1963, recording double digit wins in five consecutive seasons for the Yankees. He was traded to Oakland after the 1969 season and was off to a 3-3 start with the A's before being traded to Milwaukee. Having the veteran lefty in the rotation would hopefully be a stabilizing force and take some of the pressure off of the bullpen. Francona was one of those veteran players that provided versatility and leadership which is something the young Brewers team needed. Manager Dave Bristol said intended to use Downing as a starter in Saturday's game against the Indians and would use Francona as a pinch hitter and spot player at first base and in the outfield.

The Brewers took a 17-game road losing streak with them into Cleveland to open up their series against the Indians. Brewers' starter Marty

Pattin and Indians hurler Rich Hand both pitched shutout ball through seven innings. In the Brewers' half of the 8th, Hand issued three consecutive walks before Russ Snyder, mired in a 1 for 24 slump, launched a Grand Slam home run staking the Brewers to a 4-0 lead. Pattin would go the distance, surrendering only one run and scattering six hits to pick up his third victory of the season.

Unfortunately, in game two of the series after jumping to a quick 2-0 lead, Brewers starter Lew Krausse was battered for seven runs in one and a third innings giving the Indians a lead they would never surrender, as the Brewers lost a 10-6 slugfest. The Brewers offense continued to shine as Walton hit his 13th home run in the first inning, and Tommy Harper hit his 10th home run in the fourth inning. The bats were coming alive, but the starting pitching was still giving up too many runs for Bristol and Milkes' liking.

The Brewers would wrap up the series against the Indians with a 9-2 drubbing at the hands of the

Tribe. Indians' starter Steve Dunning, who was drafted by the Indians just one week earlier in the June amateur draft, made his professional debut. Dunning held the Brewers to just two runs on five hits over five innings to gain his first Major League victory. Brewers' starter Skip Lockwood gave up five runs on seven hits in three and a third innings before giving way to the bullpen, which surrendered an additional four runs. The loss was Milwaukee's twenty sixth on the road against only six victories. The next stop on the road trip would not be any easier as the Brewers would face the division leading Baltimore Orioles.

Before Monday's series opener against the Orioles the Brewers made several of what were expected to be many trade deadline moves, as they signed relief pitcher Bob Humphreys formerly of the Washington Senators. They then sold pitcher Bob Locker to the Oakland A's - reportedly for $75,000 and purchased former Giants outfielder Bob Burda.

On the field, the Brewers would be down 6-3 going into the top of the eighth inning against the Orioles, before exploding for six runs, the big blow being a three-run double by Roberto Pena. Ken Sanders would pick up the win, his first as a Brewer, and Dave Baldwin would pick up his first save. Both Sanders and Baldwin were sporting sub 1.00 ERAs out of the bullpen giving the Brewers a nice one two punch.

The Brewers would pull off two additional deals before the trading deadline, a minor one sending pitcher John O'Donoghue to the Montreal Expos in exchange for utility player Jose Herrera. A more important transaction was completed as the Brewers obtained outfielder Dave May from the Baltimore Orioles in exchange for minor league pitchers Dick Baney and Buzz Stephen. The 26-year-old May was a talented outfielder but was considered expendable by the Orioles as they were loaded with talent in the outfield. The lefty swinging May would slide into the departed Steve Hovley's spot in the outfield and give the Brewers a solid glove in center field.

After the Brewers' Tuesday night game against the Orioles was postponed by rain, the Brewers wrapped up the series with a Wednesday night game at Memorial Stadium. Starter Gene Brabender would go 6 1/3 innings, giving up one run and scattering seven hits, while the Brewers torched Orioles' starter Dave McNally for five runs. Phil Roof tied the game at one with a home run to left off McNally, and new Brewer Dave May drove in the go ahead run off his former mates. Mike Hegan cracked a three-run home run in the top of the seventh to round out the scoring. Newly acquired Bob Humphreys pitched two and two third innings earning his first save as a Brewer as the club triumphed 5-0.

The team would head West to face the Angels after taking two straight from the division leading Orioles and continued their winning ways as they took a 5-2 decision from the Angels. The Brewers got a strong outing from Marty Pattin with help from Bob Humphreys out of the pen, who earned his second save of the season. The hitting star of the game was catcher Phil Roof as his two-run home run put the game out of reach and help secure the 5-0 victory for the Brewers. In game two the Brewers wasted a strong outing by Lew Krausse as the bullpen surrendered three runs in the bottom of the eighth leading to a 4-0 victory by the Angels. The Brewers would lose a heartbreaker in the series finale as the bullpen twice surrendered leads and the Brewers dropped a 6-5 decision in 10 innings.

The Brewers had made several key additions to the roster prior to the trading deadline and combined with some of the call ups from AAA Portland, manager Bristol hoped to be able to stabilize the roster and string together some wins as they returned Milwaukee for a 21 game homestand that would take them into July.

CHAPTER SEVENTEEN

The Brewers returned home after their 4-7 road trip and were greeted by a crowd of 1,200 fans at Milwaukee's Mitchell Field, who were there to welcome the club home and wish them good luck on the upcoming home stand. Although the Brewers possessed the worst record in baseball, it was becoming more and more obvious that the fans in Milwaukee had accepted this team into their hearts and that the wounds felt when the Braves abandoned the city were beginning to heal.

A crowd of 18,291 showed up on a warm Monday night to watch the Brewers open the home stand against the Minnesota Twins. The Brewers took an early 1-0 lead, but starter Gene Brabender ran into trouble in the fifth inning giving up the big blow of the game, a three-run home run by Twins third baseman Harmon Killebrew. Ken Sanders came in and pitched an inning and 2/3 of hitless ball, and along with a John Gelnar, kept the Brewers in the game. The Brewers mounted a rally in the ninth inning when after single by Ted Savage, Tommy Harper hit his 12th home run of the year making the score 4-3, but that was all the Brewers could muster as the Twins took game one.

Another nice crowd turned out for game two as the Twins sent 19 year old Bert Blyleven to the mound to face Bob Bolin. Blyleven held the Brewers to one run through six innings and took a 3-1 lead into the bottom of the seventh. Phil Roof slammed a leadoff home run into the left-field stands, his sixth of the season, cutting a lead to one run. Bristol summoned Dave Baldwin from the pen and he pitched two perfect innings keeping the Brewers within striking distance heading into the ninth. The Brewers would put two runners on base when with two outs, pinch-hitter Gus Gil doubled to left, driving in two runs giving the Brewers a come-from-behind 4-3 victory. The Brewers dropped game three of the series 3-2 despite an impressive outing from Marty Pattin. Pattin pitched a complete game, scattering six hits and giving up three runs while striking out 10, but the Brewers offense could only muster two runs off of Twins' starter Dave Boswell.

The Brewers wrapped up the series with the Twins with a makeup of a May 15th rainout. With game time temperatures in the mid-50's a crowd of 7,055 watched a quick two hour and three minute victory by the Brewers. Starter Lew Krausse was brilliant, scattering four hits and striking out six as he picked up the complete-game victory. RBI's by May, Burda, and Kubiak in the bottom of the first inning accounted for all for runs the Brewers would need as Krausse only allowed an RBI single to Rich Reese in the 7th.

Oakland rolled into town for a three-game series against the Brewers, and the fans that showed up Friday night for game one certainly got their money's worth. Brewers' starter Skip Lockwood squared off against Oakland's Catfish Hunter in a marathon game that took almost four hours to complete. Oakland took a 2-0 lead in the top of the fourth and a two-run home run by Sal Bando, and the Brewers promptly got one of those runs back when Roberto Pena drove in Dave May with a sacrifice fly to center. The Brewers tied it up in the bottom of the fifth when Russ Snyder hit a solo home run off Hunter, and that would wrap up the scoring for the next 10 innings. Lockwood would give up just two hits the rest of the way finishing with a line of 12 innings pitched with two earned runs on only five hits. All totaled the Brewers rapped out 17 hits off of seven Oakland pitchers but were unable to plate another run. Finally in the bottom of the 15th inning Gus Gil lead off with a double, followed by a Mike Hershberger walk, before Dave May stroked a single scoring Gil and giving the Brewers a 3-2 walk-off victory.

A Youth Day crowd of 13,142 showed up on a beautiful Saturday afternoon and saw Brewers' starter Gene Brabender pitch a gem. The big right-hander scattered five hits giving up only one run to earn the complete-game victory. The Brewers tagged Oakland starter Rollie Fingers for three runs on five hits as they ran their winning streak to three games.

The Brewers would draw their biggest crowd since opening day for a Sunday doubleheader against the A's, and the 26,397 attendees would go home disappointed as the Brewers dropped both ends of the doubleheader by identical scores of 4-1. Game one starter Bob Bolin was only able to last four innings, giving up four runs on five hits before the bullpen combo of John Gelnar and Dave Baldwin could shut the A's down. Unfortunately for the Brewers, A's starter Diego Segui scattered seven hits through seven innings and limited the Brewers to one run, snapping the Brewers three-game winning streak. Game two starter Al Downing, making his first start since being acquired by the Brewers was rocked for 4 runs at three hits and only lasted 1/3 of an inning. Ken Sanders came out of the bullpen and pitched 7 and 2/3 innings, scattering five hits but the Brewers again we're not able to generate any offense, this time against Oakland starter Chuck Dobson. The Brewers would not have much time to reflect on the doubleheader sweep, as the California Angels would be coming to town on Monday to start a four-game series.

The Angels jumped on Brewers starter Marty Pattin early and by the fifth inning the Brewers were down 8-1 in game one. The bullpen surrendered two more runs while the Brewers were able to tack on two more and the result was a 10-3 loss to California. The lone bright spot for the Brewers was right fielder Tommy Harper who went 3 for 5 and hit his 13th home run of the season to deep left field. In game two Lew Krausse would give up three first inning runs to the Angels before getting two of those back on a two-run single by Jerry Mc Nertney in the bottom of the inning. Krausse would settle down and in the bottom of the third, Danny Walton launched his 14th home run of the season, a 392 foot blast to deep left field, tying the score at three. Krausse held the Angels scoreless until the bottom of the eighth when Walton would crush his second home run of the game to deep left field giving the Brewers a 5-3 lead. Krausse started the ninth and gave up singles to Jim Spencer and Ken McMullen before being replaced by Bob Humphreys. Humphreys will allow a single to Joe Azcue, loading the bases before getting Jay Johnstone to line out to first. The Angels cut the lead to one as Bill Voss drove in Spencer making the score 5-4. Humphreys would get Sandy Alomar to ground out 6-3 to end the inning and the Brewers walked away with an exciting 5-4 victory.

The Brewers finished the month of June with a 26 - 48 record but there were bright spots along the way. While the starting pitching was still erratic, the bullpen was much improved, especially with the additions of Baldwin and Sanders who were both sporting ERAs under 2.00. General Manager Marvin Milkes upgraded the defense with the additions of Roberto Pena and Dave May, while Tommy Harper had raised his average to .301 and found his power stroke during the month of June. The weather was warming up in Milwaukee and the fans were coming out with the Brewers halfway through the longest home stand of the season. With the All-Star break coming up the Brewers had several potential candidates, with Harper and Walton the most likely candidates, and the club was looking to go into the break on a positive note.

CHAPTER EIGHTEEN

The Brewers opened the month of July the same way they closed out the month of June, with a one-run ballgame. This time the Angels were the victors taking a 4-3 decision from the Brewers. The Angels took a 1-0 lead in the top of the second when third baseman Ken McMullen drove in Alex Johnson with a sacrifice fly to right, making the score 1-0. The Brewers would take the lead in the bottom of the second as Bob Burda hit his first homerun as a Brewer, a shot off of Andy Messersmith to deep right field, and Phil Roof drove in a run on a fielder's choice. The lead would hold up until the top of the seventh when Bill Voss singled to center driving in Jay Johnstone. Jim Fregosi would hit a two-run home run to deep left field giving the Angels at 4-2 lead. The Brewers would come back in the bottom of the seventh as Danny Walton singled in Dave May to make the score 4-3, but that's all the Brewers could muster off of Angels' relief pitcher Eddie Fisher and the club dropped a 4-3 decision.

A crowd of 12,099 came out on a scorching hot and humid afternoon and witnessed a slugfest between the Brewers and Angels. The Brewers struck first as Tommy Harper took Angels' starter Tom Murphy's first pitch deep to left field, giving the Brewers a quick 1-0 lead. The Angels would take the lead in the 2nd inning on a two-run single by Joe Azcue making the score 2-1. A run-scoring single by Phil Roof would tie the game at two, and the score stayed that way until the top of the sixth when a Jim Spencer single to right scored Jim Fregosi giving the Angels a 3-2 lead. The real damage was done in the top of the seventh as the Angels scored five runs on six hits giving the Angels an 8-2 lead. The Brewers would come back in the bottom of the seventh as Phil Roof launched a solo home run to deep left off of Murphy, and Mike Hegan laced a two-run double to left field cutting the score to 8-5. The Angels would get two of those runs back on a run-scoring double by Jim Fregosi and a fielder's choice from Jim

Spencer, making the score 10-5. The Brewers would attempt to mount a comeback in the bottom of the ninth as Tommy Harper hit his second home run of the game to deep left field cutting the score to 10 - 7. The Brewers brought the tying run to the plate with two outs, but Roberto Pena popped out to second base to end the game, giving the Angels a 10-7 victory.

The Brewers returned to action on Friday welcoming the Kansas City Royals to town for a Friday night twin-bill. Brewers starter Marty Pattin looked sharp early, holding the Royals scoreless through six as the Brewers built a 3-0 lead. Pattin would give up one run in the seventh inning and one in the top of the ninth before giving way to Bob Humphreys. With the Brewers holding a 3-2 lead Humphreys gave up a single to Tommy Matchick, tying the game at three. The game was tied at three in the top of the 10th when the Royals would plate two runs, and Ted Abernathy shut the Brewers down in the bottom of the 10th giving Kansas City a 5-3 victory in game one of the doubleheader.

In game two the Royals jumped out to a quick 1-0 lead, but the Brewers answered back when Tommy Harper led off the inning with a home run to deep left-center field. It was Harper 16th home run of the season and his sixth leadoff home run for the Brewers. A two-run single by Pat Kelly in the top of the second was countered by a two-run double from Mike Hegan in the bottom of the second tying the score at three. Both pitchers worked quickly through the sixth, and with two outs in the top of the seventh Pat Kelly would homer to deep right field off of Al Downing, giving the Royals a 4-3 lead. Both team's bullpens shut the door, and the Royals had the sweep of the doubleheader with a 4-3 victory before a crowd of 29,661.

A cool, cloudy and windy July 4th held Saturday night's crowd down to a little over 9,600 as the Brewers once again fell short against the Royals. Starter Lew Krausse didn't make it out of the second inning, giving up four runs on six hits putting the Brewers in a 4-0 hole. The Brewers would come back with three in the bottom of the fifth when Mike

Hegan stroked his sixth home run of the year and Danny Walton registered a run-scoring single to left. The Royals would add to their lead in the bottom of the sixth on a run-scoring single from Amos Otis. The Brewers tacked on one in the bottom of the sixth, and Tommy Harper would give the Brewers their first lead with a two-run single to left off of Royals' reliever Ted Abernathy. In the top of the ninth, Lou Piniella socked a three-run home run giving the Royals and 8-6 lead and Abernanthy shut the door on the Brewers in the bottom of the ninth, extending the Brewers' losing streak to five.

Sunday afternoon's series finale saw Skip Lockwood spin a gem, needing only 99 pitches to shut down the Royals, giving up one run on four hits while striking out four. Lockwood and Royals' starter Bill Butler both pitched efficiently with both Brewer RBIs credited to Gus Gil on back-to-back sacrifice flies to right field. The game was played in a crisp one hour and fifty nine minutes before a crowd of 10,323 at County Stadium as Lockwood picked up his first major league victory. Lockwood had originally come up as an infielder in the A's organization, and at 23 years old was seeing his first extended action as a pitcher in the Major Leagues. Lockwood had pitched well thus far, but had been the victim of some bad luck, and his 1-5 record was not indicative of the potential that he possessed. Manager Dave Bristol and pitching coach Wes Stock were counting on the young righty to continue to improve and become a key member of the Brewers starting rotation.

The Brewers wrapped up the long home stand with a five-game series against the White Sox, which included a makeup of an April 19th rainout. Game one pitcher Gene Brabender went the distance, giving up one run and scattering eight hits while contributing to his own cause with a run-scoring double in the bottom of the second. The only other offense for the game came from Dave May in the bottom of the sixth. Chicago pitcher Gerry Janeski fired an inside slider to May who belted it into the bleachers for his second home run of the season, giving the Brewers the lead. *"I was looking for anything inside because Janeski was pitching me tight"* said May. That was only his third hit in the last 26 at bats and May said *"Sure I've been in a slump, but I've been coming out every day and hitting about 25 minutes extra. Anyway I was worried about the slump but manager Dave Bristol went with me when I was 0 for 12 and he said I'd come out of it pretty good."*

The 15,280 fans that came out for Tuesday night's doubleheader against the White Sox certainly got their money's worth. In game one, the Brewers jumped out to a 3-0 lead in the third inning as Mike Hershberger cracked a three run home run off of White Sox starter Jim Magnuson. Brewers' starter Marty Pattin was cruising along until the top of the sixth when he gave up a two-run single to Carlos May making the score 3 - 2. In the top of the seventh Sox shortstop Luis Aparicio drove in Ken Berry on a fielder's choice tying the score at three. Pattin continued on the mound for the Brewers before being lifted for a pinch-hitter in the bottom of the 12th. With two outs, pinch-hitter Ted Savage hammered a Wilbur Wood knuckle ball over the fence giving the Brewers a dramatic 4-3 walk-off victory. Pattin would pitch all 12 innings, giving up three runs and striking out six while scattering 11 hits. Game two must have seemed to pass in the blink of an eye compared to the marathon of game one, as Lew Krausse shut down the White Sox on four hits, striking out six as the Brewers took a 1-0 decision in a game lasting only one hour and thirty four minutes. The only run of the game scored on a throwing error by White Sox pitcher Joe Horlen which allowed Mike Hegan the score from second base. The Brewers saw their winning streak stretched to four games on the back of four strong outings from the starting rotation which had to be good news for Bristol and the coaching staff.

Game four of the series pitted Chicago lefty Tommy John against Brewers' lefty Al Downing. Downing and John engaged in a scoreless pitcher's duel through seven innings, but in the 8th as Downing was covering first base he dropped a flip from first baseman Tito Francona, allowing the first White Sox run to score, making it a 1-0 contest. As a result Downing gave up two runs, neither of them earned, to drop his sixth decision of the year. The Brewers' only offense came on a sacrifice by Ted Savage that scored Dave May making the score 2-1. Tommy John went the distance for the White Sox shutting the Brewers down ending their win streak at four.

The Brewers wrapped up their series with the White Sox and the home stand with a 6-5 loss. The Brewers were down 6-2 after five innings but started chipping away at the White Sox lead scoring one in the seventh on a Tommy Harper sacrifice. In the ninth inning the Brewers brought the crowd of 14,288- most of whom were still hanging around - to their feet. Tommy Harper singled, Mike Hegan walked and Dave May singled to bring in a run. Hegan then scored on two wild pitches bringing the Brewers within one run. A pop out and a long fly to the outfield ended the threat, ball game and the home stand. Starter Skip Lockwood was rocked for six runs in 4 and 2/3 innings before the bullpen trio of Gelnar, Humphreys, and Sanders shut the White Sox down on three hits the remainder of the way.

The Brewers finished the long home stand with 9 wins and 12 losses but were playing exciting baseball which is evidenced by the crowds they were drawing. After 44 games, a little more than half the home schedule, the Brewers had drawn 508,530 fans which no doubt had to please Bud Selig and the ownership group. The team would make a quick three game jaunt to Oakland before the All-Star break with growing fan interest and high hopes for the future.

The Brewers took game one of the series as starter Bob Bolin pitched his best game of the season, giving up one run while scattering eight hits as the Brewers took a 2-1 decision handing the A's their fifth straight defeat. Oakland came back in game two and hammered the Brewers for eleven runs, six off of starter Gene Brabender and an additional five off of John Gelnar in an 11-1 trouncing of the Brewers.

The Brewers and A's wrapped up the first half of the season with a Sunday doubleheader at the Oakland-Alameda Coliseum. Oakland scored one in the first and one in the second and carried a 2-0 lead into the top of the seventh when Jerry Mc Nertney hit a two-run home run off of a starter Chuck Dobson to tie the score at two. The Brewers would take the lead in the top of the ninth as Dave May launched a home run off of Oakland reliever Paul Lindblad to give the Brewers a 3-2 to lead. In the bottom of the ninth Marty Pattin gave up a home run to Don Mincher and a run-scoring single to John Donaldson giving Oakland a 4-3 come-from-behind victory. In game two, Oakland sent Catfish Hunter up against Brewers starter Lew Krausse. Oakland scored first when Bert Campaneris homered off of Krausse to give Oakland a 1-0 lead. The score stayed that way until the top of the fourth, when Tommy Harper hit his seventh leadoff home run of the season off of Hunter, and Tito Francona grounded to second scoring Russ Snyder, giving the Brewers a 2-1 lead. That would be it for the scoring as Krausse settled down and went the distance for the Brewers, giving up one run while scattering six hits and wrapping up the first half of the season for the Brewers. The team was heading into the all-star break with a 32 - 57 record on the season as optimism was still high among the fans and front office.

CHAPTER NINETEEN

The 1970 Major League Baseball All-Star game was played in Cincinnati's brand new Riverfront Stadium. The Brewers lone representative was third baseman Tommy Harper. The leading vote-getter at second base was Minnesota's Rod Carew, but he would miss the game due to injury. The second-place vote-getter, Detroit's Dick McAuliffe would also miss the game due to injury. The starting nod should have gone to the third-place vote-getter Tommy Harper, but American League manager Earl Weaver named Dave Johnson as his starter for the Midsummer Classic. No doubt Weaver selected Johnson because he was the starting second baseman in Baltimore, but Harper's stats make a stronger case. Harper was batting .311 with 17 home runs at 40 RBIs in addition to leading the American League with 28 stolen bases. "Tailwind Tommy" certainly earned the starting nod, but he still would make the roster as a reserve.

Harper would appear as a pinch-runner in a game that would go down as an All-Star classic. The American League was leading 4-1 in the bottom of ninth when the National League scored three runs to tie the game and send it into extra innings. Cubs' outfielder Jim Hickman singled in the bottom of the 12th inning scoring Pete Rose who plowed over Cleveland Indians catcher Ray Fosse to score the winning run. Fosse ended up in a Cincinnati hospital after the game and although it was not known at the time that collision quite possibly derailed his promising career. Fosse suffered a shoulder injury and never reached his All-Star status again.

Brewers fans woke up to news Thursday morning reported by the Milwaukee Sentinel that the Brewers and Washington Senators were discussing a deal that would send Danny Walton and two pitchers to Washington for their big slugger Frank Howard. The rumored trade would occur at the end of the season and Senators owner Robert Short was quoted as saying that *"his club and Milwaukee will make a major deal at the end of the season that will put the Brewers in a contending position."* Brewers' general manager Marvin Milkes confirmed that he had spoken to Short but was non-committal on the trade. Howard, a native of Green Bay, Wisconsin wielded one of the most powerful bats in all of baseball, and the thought of the "Capital Punisher" in a Brewer uniform had to excite the fan base.

As the Brewers headed into the second half Bristol and the coaching staff had settled on an everyday lineup for the most part, and the early season roster moves were paying dividends. The acquisition of Roberto Pena helped solidify the infield defense and the May call ups of Ken Sanders and Dave Baldwin gave the Brewers one of the better bullpens in the American League. The starting pitching was still troublesome for Bristol, but the last week prior to the break saw some solid outings from the rotation.

The Brewers opened the second half with a seven game eastern road trip beginning with a three-game series against the Red Sox at Fenway Park. The

Brewers would drop a 6-5 slugfest to the Red Sox in spite of home runs from Walton, Mc Nertney, and Harper. Starter Skip Lockwood lasted only 3 and 1/3 innings giving up five runs on nine hits, but the trio of Humphreys, Sanders, and Baldwin kept the Brewers in the game until they tied it with two runs in the top of the ninth inning on Tommy Harper's eighteenth home run of the season. Bob Bolin, working in his second inning of relief got into trouble immediately in the 10th inning, giving up a single to Carl Yastrzemski, a double to Tony Conigliaro and an intentional walk to Rico Petrocelli to load the bases. Third baseman George Scott hit a fly ball deep enough to right field to score Yastrzemski giving the Red Sox a one-run victory.

In spite of a four for five performance by Tommy Harper, the starting pitching once again let the Brewers down as they dropped an 8-2 decision to the Red Sox. The Brewers carried a 1-0 lead into the bottom of the fifth inning when the first two Red Sox batters reached base when Billy Conigliaro drove them in with a triple to right. Two batters later Red

Sox pitcher Sonny Siebert singled home Conigliaro giving the Red Sox a 3-1 lead. Conigliaro would sting the Brewers once again in the bottom of the sixth when his single to left scored Petrocelli. Two batters later another Red Sox pitcher, this time Carl Koonce drove in a run on a sacrifice fly making it 5-1. The Red Sox would add three more in the bottom of the seventh, all scoring on a triple by Dick Schofield wrapping up the scoring for the day and giving the Red Sox the victory in game two of the series

The Brewers bats came alive in the final game of the series and they were able to salvage a 10-5 victory to wrap up their trip to Boston. Brewers' starter Lew Krausse struggled for seven innings giving up five runs on eight hits, but the offense bailed him out in the late innings. Mike Hegan scored on a Ted Kubiak double to right field, and Tommy Harper hit his 19th home run of the season, a two-run blast to right-center field, giving the Brewers at 6-5 lead. The Brewers would salt the game away in the ninth when Ted Kubiak launched a grand slam home run to deep right-center field giving the Brewers at 10-5 lead. Ken Sanders would work around a two-out walk in the bottom of the ninth earning his first save as a Brewer.

The Brewers moved on to Washington for a quick two-game series with the Senators. The Brewers wasted a strong performance by starter Marty Pattin and dropped another one run decision 4-3. Washington took the lead in the second inning on a two-run home run by catcher Paul Casanova. The Brewers tacked on one run in the fifth on a sacrifice by Tommy Harper and tied it up in the top of the sixth on Roberto Pena's run-scoring single to left. The Brewers grabbed the lead briefly in the top of the eighth inning on Ted Savage's sixth home run of the year. The Senators came back in the bottom of the eighth inning and tied the game on Aurelio Rodriguez's one-run single the left. This time the Brewers bullpen let them down as Bob Humphreys loaded the bases in the bottom of the ninth and Lee Maye poked a single to centerfield giving the Senators a 4-3 victory.

Prior to the game the Brewers placed reliever Dave Baldwin on the 21 Day DL, further the weakening a bullpen that was already missing John Morris and Bob Meyer. The Brewers were down to only nine healthy pictures on the staff and were searching for reinforcements both in and out of the organization.

The Brewers wrapped up their quick two gamer with the Senators with Al Downing throwing his best game as a Brewer. Despite giving up only two runs on two hits, Downing was saddled with the loss as the Brewers offense could not get untracked. Downing struck out nine and walked only one, but once again was let down by lack of run support.

The Brewers moved on to New York to face the Yankees for a brief two-game series before heading back home. The Brewers carried a 2-0 lead into the bottom of the fifth inning when starter Skip Lockwood issued two walks to open the inning. The Yankees would add two runs on a Horace Clarke sacrifice and a single to center by Jerry Kenney. Lockwood would only give up 4 hits through 5 and

2/3 innings, but would struggle with walks, issuing five which led to four Yankee runs. Despite rapping out ten hits the Brewers were only able to plate two runs, falling to the Yankees 4-2. The Brewers got back on the winning track the next day as they pounded out ten hits en-route to a 4-1 victory over the Yankees. Bob Bolin went the distance giving up one run and scattering six hits, while back to back home runs by Ted Savage and Bob Burda in the top of the fifth inning were all the offense the Brewers needed.

The Brewers enjoyed a much deserved off day as they headed back to Milwaukee to open a 10-game home stand. First up was a return engagement with the Boston Red Sox. A crowd of 20,294 gathered to watch Lew Krausse square off with Ray Culp in game one of the series. The Brewers took the lead in the bottom of the first inning on a two-run single from Roberto Pena. That lead lasted until two outs in the top of the second when Jerry Moses launched a three run home run to deep left field giving the Red Sox a 3-2 lead. Brewer nemesis Billy Conigliaro tagged Krausse for a leadoff home run in the top of the fourth extending Boston's lead. The Brewers tied it up in the bottom of the fifth when Roberto Pena laced a two-run single to center scoring Savage and Burda. Krausse settled down the rest of the way, and in the bottom of the seventh Dave May broke the tie when he crushed a two-run home run to deep right field. The Brewers tacked on two insurance runs in the bottom of the eighth on a Russ Snyder single to center scoring Krausse and Harper. Krausse would navigate around two singles in the top of the ninth before shutting the door on the Red Sox, giving the Brewers the 8-4 victory and evening his record at 10-10 for the season.

Marty Pattin turned in another strong outing in game two, surrendering only a two-run home run to Carl Yastrzemski. Pattin relied on his slider most of the game, keeping the Red Sox hitters off-balance and striking out six while going the distance. Once again the Brewers struck first in the bottom of the first inning, Harper led off with a single, and Mike Hegan hit a two-run home run to deep right field, giving the Brewers a quick 2-0 lead. Three batters later Dave May grounded into a double play allowing Ted Savage to score, giving the Brewers a 3-0 lead. Pattin shut down the Red Sox in order the next two innings and then in the bottom of the third, Tommy Harper would lead off with this 20th home run of the season to extend the Brewers lead. Pattin's only hiccup was in the top of the fourth when he surrendered the home run to Yastrzemski, but he then settled down the rest of the way. A run-scoring sacrifice by Ted Savage in the fifth and a sacrifice bunt scoring Roberto Pena in the sixth rounded out the scoring as the Brewers won their second straight game against the Red Sox 6-2.

A Sunday afternoon crowd of almost 30,000 came out hoping to see the Brewers complete the sweep of the Red Sox. Instead they watched Red Sox hitters hammer five Brewers pitchers for 12 runs and 14 hits on way to a 12-5 blowout. The Brewers defense did them no favors as they committed three errors behind the beleaguered Brewers pitchers. The bright spot for the day was Tommy Harper, who hit his 21st home run of the season in the third inning and raised his average to .321 for the season. Catcher Jerry McNerney hit his sixth home run as his average hovered around the .270 mark. The Brewers were getting good production out of their catching tandem of Mc Nertney and Phil Roof and it was proving to be one of the strong spots on the roster. In spite of the hot, humid weather a total of 72,000 fans showed up for the weekend series against the Red Sox, raising the Brewers season attendance to almost 600,000.

After an off-day on Monday the Brewers returned to action for the first of three against the Washington Senators. Al Downing got the start for Milwaukee and he tossed a spectacular game, allowing only two hits and one lone run as he notched his first win as a member of the Brewers. The game was scoreless until the top of the sixth when a Frank Howard sacrifice drove in Washington's only run of the game giving the Senator's a 1-0 lead. The Brewers countered in the bottom of the sixth as Tommy Harper remained on a tear, hitting his 22nd of the home run of the season tying the score at one. Run-scoring singles by Phil Roof and Ted Kubiak extended the Brewers lead to 3-1, and Roberto Pena would add a pair in the bottom of the eighth with a two-run single. Downing retired the side in the ninth and the Brewers would have the 5-1 victory.

Washington starter Dick Bosman handcuffed the Brewers on just five hits as the Senators took the Wednesday evening contest 4-2. Brewers starter Lew Krausse went seven innings, giving up four runs on nine hits with the big blow of the game being Frank Howard's massive two-run homer to deep left field. Krausse gave up a solo shot to Mike Epstein in the eighth extending the score to 3-2 and Rick Reichardt singled in a run to end the scoring. After the game the Brewers recalled outfielder Bernie Smith from Portland of the Pacific Coast League. Smith was hitting .332 with 13 home runs and 49 runs batted in and he will take the roster spot of pitcher Dave Baldwin who has been on the 21 day disabled list. Smith would give the Brewers another bat off the bench and provide manager Bristol with additional lineup options.

The Brewers closed out the series with the Senators by capturing a 6-2 win. Marty Pattin and Washington starter George Brunet kept the game scoreless until the bottom of the fifth when the slumping Danny Walton, in the starting lineup for the first time in over a week, led off the Brewers' half of the fifth with a single. After a walk to Mc Nertney, Roberto Pena moved the runners over to second and third bringing up Dave May. May grounded into a fielder's choice, scoring Walton and giving the Brewers the first run of the game. After an intentional walk to Ted Kubiak, Pattin hit a little pop fly single to center field scoring Mc Nertney and moving Kubiak the third. Tommy Harper would strike out to end the inning with the Brewers holding a 2-0 lead.

Pattin retired the side in the top of the sixth, and in the bottom of the six after a walk and hit by pitch, Danny Walton doubled to left-field scoring

Hegan and Savage putting the Brewers up 3-0. Roberto Pena flew out center field scoring Savage giving the Brewers a 4-0 lead. The Brewers would strike again in the bottom of the seventh on a single by Harper, who reached second on a balk by Horacio Pina. Mike Hegan hit a ground ball that was bobbled by second baseman Bernie Allen allowing the run to score. Ted Savage would follow with a single to center field scoring Hegan making the score 6-0. The Senators would finally get to Pattin in the top of the 8th, after leadoff single by Paul Casanova and infield single to Del Unser, Lee Maye singled to centerfield driving in Washington's first run. The next batter Frank Howard flew out the deep center field scoring Unser from third base and that wrapped up the scoring for the game. Ken Sanders retired the side in the top of the ninth to give the Brewers a 6-2 victory and a series win against Ted Williams' ballclub.

The Brewers would wrap up the month of July with a Twilight doubleheader against the New York Yankees. After a thirty five minute rain delay,

Bob Bolin and the Brewers were cruising along with a 3-0 lead, courtesy of a run-scoring triple from Phil Roof and Tommy Harper's 23rd home run of the season off of Yankees starter Stan Bahnsen. But the floodgates would open in the top of the seventh as Bolin walked the first two batters he faced, and then gave up a run-scoring double to Jerry Kenney and a run-scoring single to Gene Michael before being replaced by Ken Sanders. The first batter that Sanders faced, Pete Ward laced a single to center field scoring Kenney, while the next batter Horace Clarke, would fly out to center field scoring Michael. A run-scoring double to Thurman Munson followed by another run-scoring double to Bobby Murcer brought Roy White to the plate. White was issued an intentional walk and the next batter, Danny Cater, laced a single scoring Murcer and ending Sanders' night. John Gelnar would come in to retire Curt Blefary for the last out of the inning, but the damage was done, as the Yankees scored seven runs on six hits taking a 7-3 lead. Yankee reliever Lindy McDaniel and Brewer reliever John Gelnar would pitch scoreless ball the rest of the way, and the Brewers dropped game one of the doubleheader to the Yankees.

In game two, Brewers' starter Gene Brabender struggled from the beginning, giving up two runs on four hits in the first inning and another two runs in the top of the third inning, drawing boos from the crowd of 18,861. Yankees starter Fritz Peterson held the Brewers to three runs and seven hits as the Brewers scored single tallies the first and the bottom of the fifth. The highlight of the evening for the Brewers came in the bottom of the seventh when leadoff hitter Phil Roof hit a towering home run to deep left field that clanged off the foul pole, cutting the score to 5-3 Bob Humphreys would finish up the eighth and ninth inning for the Brewers as they dropped a doubleheader to the Yankees and wrapped up the month of July.

The Brewers would go 12-18 for the month of July, and although their won/loss record did not reflect it, the club was showing improvement on all fronts. The bullpen had solidified, although they did miss Baldwin while he was on the disabled list, and the starting rotation was getting stronger. Tommy Harper picked up where he left off at the All-Star break and ended of the month with a .320 batting average to go along with 22 home runs. The weather was also in the club's favor as two long home stands to start and end the month saw the club drawing some of their best crowds of the season. Going into August, the team was looking to improve and continue to draw fans to the ballpark.

CHAPTER TWENTY

The Brewers opened up the month of August by dropping a 4-1, 12 inning decision to the Yankees. Brewers' starter Al Downing and Yankees' hurler Mel Stottlemyre were locked in a pitching duel through six innings. With the score tied at one in the top of the seventh Downing's elbow began tightening up, and Dave Bristol went to Ken Sanders out of the bullpen. The Brewers had taken an early lead in the bottom of the third when Tommy Harper singled home Gus Gil to give the Brewers a 1 - 0 lead. The Brewers' lead held until the top of the seventh, when Thurman Munson doubled home Gene Michael to tie the score at one. Stottlemyre and Sanders put up goose eggs through the bottom of the 10th inning as the score remained tied at one. Bristol went to Bob Humphreys out of the bullpen in the top of the 11th and the righty held the Yankees scoreless. In the top of the 12th Humphreys ran into trouble after issuing four consecutive walks giving the Yankees a to 2-1 lead. Humphreys was replaced by John Gelnar and the next batter, Gene Michael laid down a suicide squeeze scoring Blefary from third base with the bases still loaded. The next batter Jim Lyttle would fly out to center field scoring Murcer and wrapping up the scoring. Lindy McDaniel would pitch a 1-2-3 ninth inning giving the Yankees the 4-1 victory.

The Brewers wrapped up the home stand with a Sunday afternoon tilt against the Yankees in front of 20,365 fans on an 86 degree afternoon. The Yankees got on the board first, scoring three off of starter Skip Lockwood on RBI singles by Thurman Munson, Roy White, and Danny Cater. Lockwood would settle down as the Brewers would score one in the bottom of the second and take the lead in the third. With Hegan and Savage on base Roberto Pena singled to left scoring Hegan, putting runners on first and second. Relief pitcher Mike Kekich would walk Roof loading the bases for Dave May. May singled to right field scoring Savage and Pena putting a quick end Kekich's day. Lockwood would fly out to center and the next batter, Tommy Harper, drew walk with the bases loaded scoring Phil Roof making the score 5-3. The Yankees would tie the game up in the bottom of the seventh with RBIs from Horace Clarke and Thurman Munson, closing the book on Lockwood's afternoon. The seesaw game continued in the bottom of the seventh with Roof driving in Ted Savage with an infield single, and two batters later Ted Kubiak would sacrifice, scoring Danny Walton making the score 7-5. The Brewers would add some insurance in the bottom of the eighth when Ted Savage blasted a two-run home run to deep left field while John Gelnar shut down the Yankees and the top of the ninth giving the Brewers and 9-5 victory.

In news off the field, after the game the Brewers made a minor roster move recalling right-handed pitcher Bruce Brubaker from Portland as added insurance for the pitching staff. In bigger news, the club announced that with Sunday's crowd they had surpassed the entire 1969 attendance of the club when it was based in Seattle. Through fifty nine home dates the club had drawn 678,087 fans, and with 22 home games still remaining the club had an outside shot of drawing one million fans in their first year in Milwaukee. Considering the Brewers had no off-season to pre-sell tickets, the attendance thus far was spectacular and showed that Milwaukee was indeed a big-league town!

The Brewers would hit the road for a nine-game road trip, with the first stop being Metropolitan Stadium in Minnesota for a Monday night doubleheader against the Twins. The Twins were comfortably atop the AL Western Division and had given the Brewers fits earlier in the year. The Brewers would send Marty Pattin to the mound against Minnesota's 15 game winner Jim Perry. Both pitchers threw well and the game was scoreless until the top of the fifth inning when the Brewers drew first blood on an RBI single from Jerry Mc Nertney. In the bottom of the sixth Rich Reese doubled to right field off of Pattin, scoring Tony Oliva and tying the game up at one. Reese would strike again in the bottom of the eighth as he drove a Pattin offering to second base reaching on an infield single and allowing Danny Thompson the score giving the Twins a 2-1 lead. Minnesota reliever Tom Hall would come in and pitch the ninth and strike out three to end the game, giving the Twins a one-run victory in game one of the doubleheader.

In game two the Twins sent Luis Tiant to the mound while the Brewers countered with Lew Krausse. The Brewers took the lead in the top of the first inning on a Dave May single, and never trailed as Krausse mowed down the Twins, giving up only two runs in the bottom of the ninth inning as he even his record at 11-11. The Brewers would get a two-run home run from Bob Burda, and Krausse helped himself as he singled to right left field scoring Roberto Pena as the Brewers tallied a 4-2 win and a split of the doubleheader.

In the series finale the Twins sent 19 year old left-hander Bert Blyleven to the mound, and once again he dominated the Brewers giving up two runs while striking out 12. The Twins would bomb starter

Bob Bolin for five runs over 4 and 2/3 innings, including an RBI single from Blyleven. The only offense Brewers could muster was an RBI single by Russ Snyder and an RBI double from Roberto Pena. The Brewers would move on the Chicago to take on their South Side rivals in a midweek series.

The Brewers pitching woes followed them to Chicago as the White Sox jumped on the Brewers immediately, scoring four runs in the bottom of the first and two in the bottom of the second. Starter Gene Brabender lasting an inning and 2/3, giving up six runs on four hits before being replaced by Bob Humphreys. By the time the Brewers were able to send a runner across home plate they were down 7-0 on the way to a 9-3 drubbing. The only Brewers offense came on a solo shot from Gus Gil in the sixth, and a two-run home run by Max Alvis in the seventh. Right-hander Bruce Brubaker made his Brewers debut, pitching two innings giving up two runs on two base hits and walking one batter, and after the game he was optioned back to AAA Portland. A scary moment occurred in the bottom of the fifth as White Sox third baseman Bill Melton collided with Tommy Harper on a play at third base. Harper limped off the field and was taken to a local hospital for a precautionary x-ray. Although the injury was only a bruise he was expected to be out for a short time.

Prior to Thursday's game the Brewers announced they had purchased left-handed pitcher Dick Ellsworth from the Cleveland Indians. The thirty year old Ellsworth was a ten year veteran and was expected to be used out of the bullpen giving the club another veteran arm. In game two of the series the Brewers were trailing 2-1 until the fifth inning when the White Sox pushed across five runs with only one of them being earned. Once again Al Downing was the victim of bad luck as leadoff batter Syd O'Brien struck out, but reached first on a passed ball, and later scored on a Carlos May single. Three more unearned runs scored giving the White Sox a 7-1 lead, which was all the offense they needed as the Brewers dropped their third straight, 7 - 3. Tommy Harper missed Thursday's game with a bruised thigh and was expected to be out of the lineup until Sunday, which was not good news as the Brewers could not afford to be without their most potent bat for any extended period of time. With Thursday's loss the Brewers dropped into last place in the American League Western Division for the first time since July 5th. The club would move on to Kansas City for a Friday night doubleheader against the Royals, looking to right the ship and get back on the winning track.

Tommy Harper's absence was felt as the Brewers struggled to generate any offense, dropping both games of the doubleheader in Kansas City. Royals' starter Bob Johnson shut out the Brewers over 8 and 2/3 innings and Ted Abernathy came in to record the last out of the game giving Kansas City a 4-0 win in the first game. In game two, Kansas City blew a 1-1 tie open in the bottom of the fifth scoring three runs on three hits, chasing starter Lew Krausse. The Royals would add three more in the bottom of the seventh, and three more in the bottom of the eighth off of Dick Ellsworth in his first Brewer appearance, and cruise to a 10-2 victory and a sweep of the twin bill. Uncharacteristically, the bullpen let the team down giving up six runs on nine hits in 3 and 2/3 innings. Even starter Gene Brabender saw action in relief, as the Brewers were still shorthanded in the bullpen

The Brewers would come back on Saturday night getting a strong outing from Marty Pattin, who went seven innings giving up three runs on seven hits while Ken Sanders pitched the final two for his fourth save of the season. Tommy Harper missed his third straight game, but a two run home run from Ted Savage, and an RBI double for Mike Hegan provided all the offense the Brewers would need giving them their first win of the series by a score of 5-3. The team would wrap up the series, and the road trip with a 4-2 victory over the Royals. Bob Bolin went six innings giving up two runs while Ken Sanders pitched the final three frames to record his fifth save. The hitting star of the day was Dave May as he went two for five with a two-run double as the team finished with a record of 3-6 on the road trip.

The club would be back home in Milwaukee for an eight-game home stand, including their first look at 1969 Cy Young Award winner Denny McLain, and a promotion that would see them draw their largest crowd of the year.

CHAPTER TWENTY ONE

After an off-day on Monday the Brewers returned to Milwaukee to kick-off a home stand versus the Detroit Tigers. On a beautiful Tuesday evening 15,853 fans turned out the welcome to Brewers back home. The Tigers took an early lead in the bottom of the first inning on a run-scoring single from Bill Freehan, but the Brewers got that run back in the bottom of the first inning when Ted Savage launched his 10th home run of the season tying the score at one. The score would stay tied until the top of the sixth when Don Wert ripped a Downing pitch to center field scoring Freehan, giving the Tigers a 2-1 advantage. Controversy ensued in the bottom of the sixth inning when Danny Walton hit what everybody assumed was his 17th home run of the season over the left-field fence, but was ruled foul by umpire John Rice. The call prompted a lengthy argument as manager Dave Bristol was stunned at the umpires call. Instead of a game-tying home run

Walton singled on the very next pitch, but was stranded as the Brewers could not drive him in. Al Downing pitched seven strong innings giving up only two runs, but once again was let down by a lack of run support. Ken Sanders pitched a scoreless eighth and ninth inning, but the Brewers were not able to plate another run, dropping a 2-1 decision the Tigers.

On Wednesday night the bullpen and the bench came through for the Brewers in game two. The Tigers tagged Lew Krausse for five runs over 5 and 1/3 innings giving them a 5-2 lead. The Brewers bats came alive and the bottom of the eighth inning on a walk by Mike Hegan, and a single to left by Ted Savage. Danny Walton singled to left scoring Hegan and advancing Savage to third. Savage would score on an error by Tigers' second baseman Dick McAuliffe, leaving runners on second and third. Pinch hitter Tito Francona drew an intentional walk, and Dave Bristol went to his bench bringing in right-handed-hitting Bernie Smith to bat for May. Smith ripped a double to right-field driving in Snyder and

Pena giving the Brewers the lead. Bob Bolin shut the Tigers down in the ninth inning giving the Brewers a 6-5 victory.

The Brewers wrapped up their series with Detroit with a Thursday afternoon matchup. Marty Pattin would take the mound for the Brewers facing the defending Cy Young Award winner Denny McLain. McLean was considered the best pitcher in baseball the past two seasons, winning 31 games in 1968 and capturing the Cy Young Award while leading the Tigers to the World Series championship. Mc Lain would come back in 1969 winning 24 games and once again being named the Cy Young Award winner, this time in a tie with Baltimore's Mike Cuellar. While McLain was a superstar on the field, his off-field activities cost him dearly. When it was discovered that McLain was involved in bookmaking activities he was suspended indefinitely by baseball commissioner Bowie Kuhn. After the suspension was reduced to the first three months of the season Mc Lain returned in July to the Tigers staff, but struggled to regain his prior form.

The crowd of almost 20,000 on a 90-degree afternoon booed McLain lustily as he took the mound in the bottom of the first, already holding a 2-0 lead. Although Mc Lain did not have his Cy Young stuff he was able to get through the first three innings scattering two hits and a walk. The Brewers would get to McLain in the bottom of the fourth inning as Bob Burda led off the inning with a double to right. After a Danny Walton groundout, Roberto Pena tripled to right field scoring Burda. The next batter, Phil Roof laid down a suicide squeeze to the pitcher, reaching base when nobody covered first scoring Pena and tying the game at two. Brewer starter Marty Pattin had settled down after giving up two runs in the first inning and retired the Tigers in order in the top of the fifth. Dave May lead off the bottom of the fifth inning and crushed a McLain offering to deep right field giving the Brewers a 3-2 lead. McLain would give up a single to Danny Walton, and elicited boos from the crowd once again when he threw over to first base eight consecutive times, attempting to pick Danny Walton off base.

Pena would fly out to center and Walton would get caught stealing at second base ending the inning with the Brewers up 3-2.

McLain would be lifted for a pinch-hitter in the eighth inning while Marty Pattin would cruise the rest of the way for the Brewers, tossing a complete-game five-hitter and evening his record at 9-9. Thursday afternoons' crowd brought the total attendance for the year up to 731,565, for an average of 13,064 per game. To draw a crowd of almost 20,000 on a hot Thursday afternoon is a testament to the Milwaukee baseball fans and a sign of good things to come.

After the game it was announced that the Brewers had sold first baseman Greg Goossen to the Washington Senators. The twenty-four-year-old Goosen was batting .301 for Portland with 20 home runs and would be reporting directly to the major league club. The circumstances surrounding Goosen's demotion in mid-May and subsequent sale are somewhat cloudy. Goosen was batting .283

when he was demoted, and hit .309 the year before in limited duty with the Pilots. Certainly the Brewers could have used a strong right-handed bat at first base at a time when the offense was struggling. During a conversation with Goossen's brother Dan in 1989 I asked him why Greg was sent down and he suggested that an altercation between his brother and manager Dave Bristol resulted in Goossen's demotion and subsequent sale.

Cleveland came to town to open up a two-game weekend series against the Brewers. In an odd scheduling quirk to accommodate the Green Bay Packers, there would be no game on Saturday as the Packers were scheduled to meet the Chicago Bears in the annual Midwest Shrine game, played each year at County Stadium.

The Indians scored first on a run-scoring single from Ray Fosse off of Brewers' starting pitcher Skip Lockwood. The Brewers would take the lead in the bottom of the second on a two-run single by Tommy Harper and a run scoring sacrifice fly by

Mike Hegan. The Indians would tie the score in the top of the fourth when Jack Heidemann singled in Eddie Leon, and Roy Foster hit a sacrifice fly to center scoring Heidemann. The score remained tied as both bullpens took the game into the 11th inning. Pinch hitter Tito Francona led off the inning with a double into the right-field corner. Max Alvis came in to pinch run for Francona and was sacrificed to third base by Kubiak. Pinch-hitter Jerry Mc Nertney walked, putting two runners on. Tommy Harper would strikeout before by Hegan rapped a hard grounder to Eddie Leon at second base. The Indians' infielder couldn't find the handle and Alvis scored the winning run giving the Brewers the 4-3 victory. Bob Bolin, relying on his slider pitched 4 and 1/3 innings to pick up his second victory of the week. The victory also moved the Brewers into a tie with Kansas City for fourth place in the Western Division.

After the game the Brewers made another roster move as they optioned relief pitcher Bob Humphreys to AAA Portland and activated right-hander Dave Baldwin from the disabled list. Baldwin was pitching well, posting a 2-1 record with an ERA of 2.54 before he was injured in a collision at first base in Boston.

The Brewers drew their largest crowd of the season on Sunday afternoon as 44,387 fans turned out on "Bat Day" and were treated to another one run victory by the Brewers. The Indians would score two runs in the second inning as the result of a three-base error by left fielder Danny Walton. The Indians added one more run in the top of the fourth when Buddy Bradford launched a tremendous 415 foot blast into the center-field bleachers giving the Indians a 3-0 lead. The Brewers would be held scoreless until the eighth when Ted Kubiak led off the inning with a single. With one out, Tommy Harper singled and Mike Hegan walked to load the bases. Dave May bounced into a force play at home before Danny Walton crushed a double to center field driving in three and tying the game at three. In the bottom of the ninth with the score tied, Roberto Pena and Jerry Mc Nertney both walked to start the inning. Ted Kubiak sacrificed the runners to second and third and Bristol sent Gus Gil to the plate to pinch-hit for Russ Snyder. Gil delivered a seeing-eye single between third and short scoring Pena with the game-winning run giving the Brewers a sweep of the weekend series.

The fans in attendance not only witnessed an exciting ball game they got to see "Bernie Brewer" finally end his 40 day stay on top of the scoreboard. "Bernie", actually 69 year old Milton Mason, had climbed atop the 100 foot high score board on July 6th, where he was to stay until the Brewers had a crowd of 40,000. On top of the scoreboard in right center field was a house trailer, complete with a tape recorder, television and a telephone. "*I got lonesome once in a while when the team was out of town or on nights when there was a day game, but not very often,*" Bernie said. So excited was Mason to make his way down off his scoreboard perch that he descended the rope without wearing gloves, suffering rope burns on both hands as he made his way to the bottom.

The Baltimore Orioles were next on the schedule as they opened up a three-game series on Monday night against the Brewers. The Brewers were involved in their sixth straight one-run game, this time coming up on the short end 3-2. Starter Lew Krausse pitched well, going nine innings giving up only five hits, but once again the Brewers defense was their undoing. The team committed three errors in the game and one of those unearned runs proved to be the difference as Baltimore's Jim Palmer was masterful, going nine innings and giving up only three hits. The game was played in a crisp one hour and 59 minutes and Monday night's attendance of 12,015 pushed the Brewers season total over 800,000. With twenty two home games still remaining, the club stood a good chance to break the one million mark in attendance.

Game two starter Marty Pattin held the powerful Oriole offense to only three hits in eight innings, unfortunately those three hits resulted in a two run single by Boog Powell, and a mammoth home run by Merv Rettenmund, while the Brewers offense was shut out by Orioles' starter Jim Hardin. The Brewers only managed five hits wasting an outstanding effort by Pattin. 16,049 fans turned out on a humid evening to watch the Brewers and Orioles wrap up the home stand. The Brewers dropped another one run decision, this time 3-2, as starter Skip Lockwood went 7 and 2/3 innings, giving up ten hits and watching his record fall to 1-10. Orioles Lefty Mike Cuellar notched his 18th win of the season as he scattered six hits over eight innings. Cuellar had kept the Brewers hitters off-balance for most of the game as the only offense the team was able to generate was a fifth inning solo home run by Ted Kubiak, and a long home run by Mike Hegan in the bottom of the sixth. The game was tied in the top of the eighth when Merv Rettenmund singled to center field, driving in Brooks Robinson and giving the Orioles their margin of victory.

Although the Brewers had dropped three to the Orioles the home stand had to be considered a success as the team finished with a 4-4 record and drew their biggest crowds of the season. Baseball commissioner Bowie Kuhn also announced he had plans to return to Milwaukee and spend part of the evening in the left-field bleachers with the "Brew Crew" at County Stadium. Kuhn stated he planned to attend the twilight doubleheader against the Twins on September 1st. He said he has heard glowing reports about the team's progress both on the field and at the gate and wanted to see it personally. This had to be sweet news to Bud Selig and his ownership group after being thwarted several times in their attempts to bring Major League Baseball back to Milwaukee. The city and the fans were proving that Selig was right for not giving up on his dream and the fruits of those efforts were on display for all to see.

The Brewers moved on to Detroit for the start of a 10-game road trip. The Brewers took a quick 3-0 lead on the Tigers as Danny Walton tripled home Mike Hegan and Ted Savage in the top of the first inning. In the top of the second Al Downing helped his own cause singling to centerfield driving in Ted Kubiak making the score 3-0. Downing was pitching well, but once again was let down by the Brewers defense. The team committed four errors resulting in only one of Detroit's six runs being earned. Downing deserved a much better fate, he pitched 3 and 1/3 innings giving up only three hits but four unearned runs. The Brewers would battle back in the top of the fifth inning when Phil Roof hit his ninth home run of the season but that's as close as the Brewers would get as they would drop a 6-4 decision.

In game two the Brewers again faced Denny McLain, and McLain won the rematch 5 - 2. Tommy Harper led off the game with his 24th home run of the season and Dave May hit his sixth in the top of the second, but that would be it for the Brewers as McLain blanked them the rest of the way. Lew Krausse was tagged for all five runs, including two home runs, going only 4 and 1/3 innings. Dick Ellsworth and Dave Baldwin came on in relief and pitched scoreless baseball the rest of the way. The game was played in a steady rain that left the infield a swamp and manager Dave Bristol was not happy, closing the Brewers dressing-room to sportswriters after his club had lost their fifth consecutive game at Tiger Stadium.

The losing streak was extended to six games as Tiger lefty Mickey Lolich shut down the Brewers on just two hits, while striking out 14. Brewers' starter Marty Pattin pitched well, giving up only one run on five hits but the offense could do nothing against Lolich. The only offense the Brewers could muster occurred in the ninth inning when pinch-hitter Jerry Mc Nertney and Roberto Pena drew walks, and Bernie Smith was hit by a pitch to load the bases. Tiger manager Mayo Smith brought relief specialist Tom Timmermann in from the bullpen, and he got the next three batters saving the game for Lolich and giving the Tigers a 1-0 victory, and a sweep of the series.

With an off-day on Monday the Brewers made some roster news as they announced that six players from their farm system were recalled to join the parent club. Two of those players, infielder Hank Allen, and right-handed pitcher Roric Harrison would be joining the team at spring training while the other four would join the team in Milwaukee following the Pacific Coast League season which ends on September 2nd. Scheduled to join the Brewers in Milwaukee were right-handed pitchers Wayne Twitchell and Bob Humphreys, infielder Fred Stanley and outfielder/catcher Pete Koegel. Twitchell had a 9-12 record at Portland with a 5.29 ERA. Humphreys was optioned to Portland on August 14th when reliever Dave Baldwin was removed from the disabled list, and Stanley who plays shortstop and second base hit .264 while at Portland. The Brewers said Koegel, a 23-year old, six foot six, 225 lb slugger was the most exciting prospect among those recalled. He led the Southern League with 13 home runs and 51 RBIs before being promoted from Jacksonville to Portland in early July. In his first 39 games at Portland, Koegel was batting .268 with 10 home runs and 28 RBIs. Although the Brewers were not in the pennant race, the expanded roster would give them the opportunity to look at some of the younger players and start making decisions for the 1971 season.

The Brewers would open a three-game series in Cleveland with the Indians on Tuesday night, and got a strong outing from starter Skip Lockwood. Lockwood looked sharp, giving up two runs while scattering eight hits. Indian starter Sam McDowell would strikeout twelve Brewers and only gave up two runs on five hits as the game would go into extra innings. In the top of the tenth Indians' reliever Dennis Higgins would strikeout Mike Hegan, and get Russ Snyder to flyout to left field for two quick outs. Bristol opted to stick with reliever Ken Sanders at the plate, and he promptly poked a single to centerfield putting the go-ahead run on base. The next batter, Bernie Smith hit a two-run home run – his first as a Major Leaguer, giving the Brewers a 4-2 lead. Smith, who had been in organized ball since 1962, finally played in his first major league game with the Brewers on July 31st. *"It certainly rates as my biggest thrill,"* Smith said of his homer. *"To win the game is most the important thing, but to hit your first major league home run is something else."* Sanders would retire the Indians in order in the bottom of the 10th to pick up his third win of the season as the Brewers took the first game 4-2.

In game two the drama clearly occurred before the game as an anonymous telephone call to the Indians office about 30 minutes before game time stated that a bomb has been planted in Cleveland Stadium and was set to go off at 8 pm. Police immediately began a search and the game started on schedule at 7:45 after no bomb was found. The 8 p.m. deadline passed without incident and the crowd remained in the stands while police searched for the bomb, although some of the fans moved to the far left and right field sections of the stadium after those sections were searched. This was not the first bomb scare phoned into a professional sporting event, as the previous weekend several NFL games were plagued by bomb scares which turned out to be hoaxes. Bomb threats were a common occurrence in the late 1960's and early 1970's and professional sports were not immune.

As for the game, once again Al Downing would be a victim of bad luck, as he only gave up three runs in five innings, while the bullpen surrendered four runs putting the game effectively out of reach for the Brewers. The Brewers were only able to muster two runs off of Indian starter Steve Hargan, those coming on a two-run double they Mike Hegan in the top of the third inning. The star for the Indians was former Brewer farmhand Roy Foster, who drove in three runs on a fielder's choice and a two-run home run.

The Brewers offense would explode in the rubber game of the series, blasting four Indian pitchers for fourteen runs on twelve hits to take a 14-2 victory. Lew Krausse went the distance, giving up two runs on seven hits raising his record to 12-14. The Brewers scored early and often scoring one in the first and four more in the second, including Roberto Pena's second home run of the year, jumping out to a 5-0 lead. The Brewers would continue adding to the scoring as Tommy Harper cracked his 25th home run of the season, a two-run shot in the top of the fifth, and Danny Walton closed out the scoring in the ninth inning with his 17th home run of the season. The Brewers were also helped by five Indian errors in addition to eleven walks issued by a Cleveland pitching staff as they picked up the series win. The Brewers would next head to Baltimore for a four-game series, including a makeup game from June 16th, to wrap up the road trip and the month of August.

The Brewers would get another gem from Marty Pattin in the first game of the doubleheader against Baltimore. Pattin, and Orioles' starter Jim Hardin would match goose-eggs through five innings. The Brewers would finally break the scoreless deadlock with a Russ Snyder double, and after a Dave May fly out, Hardin issued an intentional walk to Mike Hegan. Danny Walton doubled to left-center field scoring Snyder and Hegan making the score 2-0, giving Pattin all the offense he would need. The Orioles would make it exciting in the bottom of the eighth when Elrod Hendricks would drive a Pattin pitch deep over the center-field fence cutting the score to 2-1. Pattin would settle down retiring the Orioles in the ninth as the Brewers took a 2-1 victory. Pattin would go all nine innings, scattering four hits and giving up one run, to bring his record to 10 - 11.

In game two the Brewers carried a 4-2 lead into the bottom of the sixth inning when the Orioles would tag the Brewers for five runs in the inning. An Elrod Hendricks sacrifice fly made the score 4- 3, and after giving up a double to Davey Johnson, Bristol pulled Gene Brabender and brought in Dave Baldwin from the bullpen. Baldwin would strikeout Chico Salmon, and issue an intentional walk to Boog Powell to face Don Buford. Buford would make Baldwin and the Brewers pay as he launched a grand slam to deep right field, making the score 7-4. The Orioles would add one more on a solo home run from Merv Rettenmund in the seventh while the Brewers were shut down the rest of the way as they dropped game two of the twin bill 8-4. After the game the Brewers announced that minor league shortstop Rick Auerbach would not be joining the team next week after suffering an injury in a Pacific Coast League game in Portland. Auerbach was injured Thursday night when he was hit with a foul tip off his own bat during a game against Spokane. Auerbach received a cut near the eye that required five stitches and a possible hairline skull fracture.

The Brewers' offense went cold in game three as Orioles' lefty Dave McNally limited the Brewers to one run on seven hits as he notched his 21st win of the season with a 6-1 victory. The only Brewers offense and the day came on a Tommy Harper single to right field that scored Bernie Smith in the top of the eighth inning. Although Harper's average had dropped just below .300 he was closing in on 30 home runs and was making a strong case as the American League Most Valuable Player. With a little more than a month left in the season many around the Brewers thought Harper had a legitimate a chance to capture the MVP award.

The Brewers wrapped up the road trip, and the month of August on a positive note as they took a 5-2 decision from the Orioles. The Brewers never trailed in the game, scoring first on Tommy Harper's 26th home run of the year, a two run shot off of Jim Palmer, giving the Brewers a 2-0 lead. After giving up a solo home run to Dave Johnson, Skip Lockwood would settle down as the Brewers would score three more runs in the top of the fifth on a home run from Mike Hegan and a run scoring double by Roberto Pena, who advanced to third on the throw home. Pena would then steal home off of Palmer giving the Brewers a 5-1 lead. The Orioles added one run in the bottom of seventh and Lockwood would pitch 7 and 2/3 innings before giving way to Ken Sanders. Sanders would shut the Orioles down the rest of the way to earn his sixth save of the year the as the Brewers earned a series split with the Orioles.

The Brewers won 12 and lost 17 games in the month of August, and although they would not be planning for the postseason, the team still had many goals within their reach. With two more home stands coming up in the month of September, the possibility that the Brewers could draw one million fans in their first year was very real and would be considered quite the accomplishment. The Brewers also had several young players coming up with the rosters expanding, giving them an opportunity to take a look at the future. The team was improving all around and there definitely was optimism going into September and the offseason.

CHAPTER TWENTY TWO

The Brewers would open the final month of the 1970 season with a record of 50 - 84. Although the team's performance on the field may have fallen below expectations, the performance off the field greatly exceeded them. The club would return home for a quick four game home stand against the Twins and White Sox, before heading out on the road for a nine-game trip.

The Brewers made news off the field when they announced outfielder Danny Walton would undergo surgery after the season to correct a dislocated kneecap. Walton would be sidelined about 10 days with this latest injury, and his leg will be in a cast most of the week. Walton re-injured the knee while rounding first base in the fourth inning of last Friday's game against Baltimore. The team also made two roster moves, first calling up utility man Hank Allen, who was with the club briefly earlier in the season. The second move, and the most interesting one, was the team announced it had signed free agent Harvey Kuenn. The 39 year old Kuenn was a native of West Allis Wisconsin, and had been out of baseball since 1966. The club added the 1953 AL rookie of the year to the active roster in order to improve Kuenn's pension situation. Although Kuenn would not see any game action, he would remain with the club in various capacities in the coming years, culminating in being named the team's manager in 1982 and leading that club to the World Series.

On the field the Brewers would play a Tuesday night doubleheader against the Twins. The Twins jumped on top first when slugger Harmon Killebrew took a Lew Krausse curveball to deep left field for a three-run homer giving the Twins a lead they would never relinquish. The Twins would add one more in the fourth on a Leo Cardenas single to right wrapping up the scoring for the night. Twins hurler Jim Perry pitched a masterful nine-innings, scattering five hits and striking out nine, while picking up his 20th win of the season. Krausse lasted six innings and saw his record drop to 12-15. In game two it would be Killebrew again who would do the most damage. Killebrew drove in a run in the first inning which would account for all of the scoring until the Brewers tied it up in the bottom of the ninth inning. With two on and two out Ted Kubiak laced a single to center field off of Jim Kaat scoring Max Alvis and tying the score at one. Both bullpens would keep it scoreless until the top of the eleventh when the Twins erupted for six runs on three hits, with Killebrew's second home run of the night plating three runs and giving the Twins a 7-1 lead. Kaat would retire the Brewers in the bottom of the eleventh, securing the victory and the sweep of the doubleheader.

Wednesday's game against the Twins was rained out and the teams would wrap up the series the following afternoon. The rainy, overcast weather continued on Thursday holding the crowd to 6,583, and as the players and fans were preparing to come to the ballpark they were learning of the death of legendary Packer coach Vince Lombardi. Lombardi had passed away early Thursday morning at the age of 57 after battling cancer for several months, and his passing was mourned throughout the sporting world.

The Brewers were in command from the beginning taking a 1-0 lead in the bottom of the second on Ted Kubiak's RBI single to right. The Brewers scored five in the bottom of the fifth inning on RBI singles from Dave May, and Roberto Pena, while catcher Phil Roof launched a three-run home run to deep left field, his 10th of the season, giving the Brewers a 6-0 lead. The Twins would finally get on the board in the top of the sixth on an RBI ground out from Danny Thompson, and tallied two more in the top of the seventh on a two-run home run by a Brant Alyea. Roberto Pena homered to left field in the bottom of the seventh, driving in two making the final tally 8-3. Marty Pattin would go 7 and 1/3 innings to even his record at 11-11, and Ken Sanders pitched the last inning and 2/3, recording his seventh save of the year.

The White Sox came to town next for a two-game weekend series against the Brewers. The flags at Milwaukee County Stadium were at half-staff as prior to the game, and the crowd of 11,953 paid a silent tribute to Vince Lombardi the former coach and general manager of the Green Bay Packers.

Once the game got underway the crowd saw a pitcher's duel between Brewers starter Skip Lockwood and the White Sox' Gerry Janeski. Both teams were blanked until the bottom of the fifth inning, when the Brewers scored two runs on an RBI single from Ted Kubiak, and a sacrifice fly from Russ Snyder making the score 2-0. The White Sox would get on the board in the top of the seventh when Gail Hopkins bounced into a fielder's choice scoring Rich Morales, bringing the White Sox within one. After two consecutive singles in the top of the eighth Lockwood was replaced by Ken Sanders. The second batter Sanders faced, Bob Spence hit into a fielder's choice, scoring Carlos May and tying the game at two. Sanders and White Sox reliever Danny Murphy pitched scoreless ball until the bottom of the 10th when Tommy Harper led off the inning with a walk and was sacrificed to second by Russ Snyder. Murphy would issue an intentional walk to Dave May and the next batter, Floyd Wicker, singled to center field scoring Tommy Harper and giving the Brewers a 3-2 walk-off victory in 10 innings.

The Brewers would have a Saturday evening off to accommodate the Green Bay Packers and their exhibition football game against the Cincinnati Bengals. Once again the weather would not cooperate and Sunday afternoon's finale against the White Sox was rained out with a make-up date set for September 25th. Unfortunately for the Brewers, this would necessitate the game being played in Chicago, costing the Brewers a home date and making their quest for one million fans more difficult.

The Brewers traveled to Minnesota to start an eight-game road trip against the Twins. The Brewers dropped both ends of the Monday night doubleheader, losing a 7-6 decision in game one.

The Twins jumped on starter Lew Krausse for seven runs in two innings, effectively putting the game out of reach, in spite of a late-game comeback attempt by the Brewers. Krausse would only last two innings while four Brewer pitchers held the Twins scoreless the rest of the way. 22 year old Wayne Twitchell made his major league debut for the Brewers and pitched one inning, striking out the side. A combination of the Twins' hot bats and the Brewers defense cost the Brewers in game two as the Twins scored three unearned runs, taking an 8-3 decision. Twins starter Luis Tiant left the game after 1 inning and was replaced by Hal Haydel, who was making his major league debut. Haydel would give up two runs on four hits over five innings and gained his first major league victory. Haydel would help his own cause with a home run and a single. The score would be 4-3 until the bottom of the seventh when the Twins with scored four runs off of Brewer reliever Bob Bolin. Three of those runs would be unearned on an error by Tommy Harper as the Twins earned the doubleheader sweep.

The Brewers wrapped up the season series with the Twins capturing an exciting 3-2 victory in Minnesota. The Brewers were down 2-1 going into the top of the ninth inning, when with two outs Phil Roof hit a two run home run to deep left field giving the Brewers a 3-2 lead. Marty Pattin would shut the door on the Twins in the bottom of the ninth inning, wrapping up an evening where he would throw a complete-game six-hitter giving up only two runs while striking out seven, improving his record to 12–11.

Kansas City would be next on the trip for the Brewers and the inclement weather followed them as Wednesday's series opener was rained out, rescheduled as part of a Thursday doubleheader. While discussing the Brewers improvements throughout the season manager Dave Bristol highlighted the pitching staff, and the bullpen in particular as he said that the bullpen had made tremendous improvement since June 15th. Bristol specifically cited Ken Sanders saying *"If we would have had him earlier in the year, we would be in fourth place right now,"* Bristol said of Sanders. The club also announced that outfielder Danny Walton would undergo knee surgery on Monday, and no doubt the loss of his big bat would hurt the lineup.

The Brewers dropped game one of the doubleheader by a score of 2-0, despite a strong effort from Skip Lockwood. Lockwood would go seven strong innings, giving up two runs on three hits while striking out five. The Brewers bats were unable to muster any offense against Royals' starter Bill Butler, who gave up three hits while striking out four over 8 and 1/3 innings pitched. The Brewers would get clobbered in game two 10-2, as back-to-back five-run innings by the Royals proved to be the Brewers' undoing. The Brewers' only offense came from a leadoff home run by Bob Burda in the top of the second, and a run-scoring sacrifice by Russ Snyder in the top of the seventh as the Brewers only managed five hits off of Royals' starter Dick Drago.

The Brewers would next head west to Anaheim for a three-game series against the Angels.

Prior to leaving for the road trip the Brewers announced that they had traded pitcher Bob Bolin to the Boston Red Sox for cash considerations and a player to be named later. The 31-year old right-hander had a record of 5-11 with a 4.91 ERA in 32 games, 20 of them starts. Bolin also had three complete games and one save in 132 innings pitched.

The Brewers received stellar pitching in game one of the series from starter Lew Krausse and the club's game-saving specialist, Ken Sanders. Krausse went 6 and 1/3 innings giving up one run on six hits, while Sanders came in and pitched the remaining 2 and 2/3 innings, slamming the door on the Angels to collect his eighth save the season. The game was scoreless until the top of the fifth, when consecutive RBI singles by Roberto Pena and Phil Roof gave the Brewers a 2-0 lead. The Angels would threaten in the bottom of the seventh inning, as Krausse gave up singles to Alex Johnson, Ken McMullen, and Tony Gonzalez to load the bases. Bristol would bring Sanders in from the bullpen and he limited the damage, allowing only a run scoring sacrifice fly by

Bill Voss before striking out Roger Repoz ending the inning leaving the score at 2-1. That would be it for the scoring as Sanders blanked the Angels the rest of the evening, and the Brewers walked away with the victory in game one.

Saturday night's game saw another fine outing from hard-luck pitcher Al Downing, as he would give up two runs at six innings while striking out three. Although Downing would not figure in the decision, the Brewers would win another exciting game 3-2, on the strength of a two run double from Ted Savage in the top of the eighth inning. John Gelnar pitched three innings of scoreless ball to collect the win, guaranteeing the Brewers at least a series win. Not all the excitement occurred on the field as a skirmish broke out in the Angels' clubhouse between an unnamed pitcher and outfielder which left the clubhouse in disarray.

The fisticuffs continued on Sunday as utility player Chico Ruiz, and outfielder Alex Johnson exchanged words and punches in a skirmish near the batting cage Sunday afternoon. Tempers were flaring after the Angels had lost their ninth straight game the day before to the Brewers, and the altercation was nothing out of the ordinary for Johnson as his behavior was making headlines most of the season. After the preliminary matches, the main event would start and the Angels would jump on Brewers' starter Marty Pattin in the bottom of the first inning as Jim Fregosi tripled home Sandy Alomar and Alex Johnson grounded into a 6-3 sacrifice scoring Fregosi. Angels starter Tom Murphy blanked the Brewers through 7 and 1/3 innings, and the Angels bullpen held the Brewers until the top of the ninth, when a Tommy Harper single scored Ted Kubiak, making the final score 2-1.

The Brewers would have an off-day on Monday before they would open their final home stand of the 1970 season with three games against the Oakland Athletics. With nine home games left the club hoped that with cooperation from Mother Nature, the fans would continue to come out and push the Brewers to the magical one million mark in attendance.

CHAPTER TWENTY THREE

The Brewers opened their final home stand of the season with a Monday night rain out of their game versus the Oakland A's. The club would pick up the series by playing a double-header on Tuesday with Skip Lockwood facing Blue Moon Odom in the first game. Lockwood was magnificent throwing his best game of the year, a two-hit complete game shutout, striking out ten batters. The only offense of the game came in the bottom of the fifth inning on a run-scoring single by Dave May.

Game two starter John Morris would last 4 and 1/3 innings giving up four runs on four hits. The Brewers offense would get to Oakland starter Vida Blue chasing him after 5 and 1/3 innings. The A's would strike first on a solo home run from Bert Campaneris in the top of the third inning. The Brewers tied the game when Bernie Smith singled driving in Ted Kubiak and the game would remain tied until top of the fifth. After Morris issued a bases-loaded walk to Joe Rudi, Bristol went to the bullpen and reliever John Gelnar gave up a fielder's choice to Felipe Alou, allowing Dick Green to score. The next batter, Tommy Davis singled driving in Joe Rudi giving Oakland a 4-1 lead. The Brewers would come back in the bottom of the sixth inning when after a leadoff walk to Bernie Smith, Ted Savage tripled scoring Smith. Tito Francona then reached on an error by the first baseman Tommy Davis allowing Savage to score. Dave Baldwin and Ken Sanders would shut down the A's in the seventh and eighth inning. In the bottom of the eighth inning Floyd Wicker singled, and after a Dave May groundout, Ted Savage cracked his 11th home run of the season off of former Brewer Bob Locker, giving the Brewers a 5-4 lead. Ken Sanders would get the first two batters in the top of the ninth before walking Dave Duncan. The next batter, Bert Campaneris hit his second home run of the game, a two-run shot giving the Athletics a 6-5 lead Jim Roland would come in to pitch the ninth for Oakland, closing the door on the Brewers and giving the A's a 6-5 come-from-behind victory.

In the final game of the series the Brewers faced emergency starter Rollie Fingers. Oakland's scheduled starter, Diego Segui developed a blister and Fingers was pressed into service. Fingers, making his first start since August 12th, stymied the Brewers pitching a complete game, scattering eight hits and only giving up one run. Fingers helped his own cause in the top of the ninth when he hit a leadoff home run off Brewer reliever John Gelnar on the way to the Athletics registering a 4-1 victory over the Brewers. The only scoring for the Brewers came on Phil Roof's 12th home run of the season in the bottom of the second inning. Game time temperatures in the upper 50's kept attendance down to 6,161, which was about half of what the Brewers would need to average the rest of the way if they were to reach their goal of one million in paid attendance.

Kansas City would make their final appearance of 1970 at County Stadium and the 7,116 that turned out for game one of the four-game series certainly got their money's worth. The Brewers took a 2-0 lead on Dave May's two run home run in the bottom of the first inning, his eighth of the year. The Royals would get one of those runs back in the top of the second with Lou Piniella took a Marty Pattin pitch deep over the left-field fence cutting the score to 2-1. Pattin, and Royals' starter Dick Drago would pitch scoreless ball until the top of the sixth, when Royals' catcher Ed Kirkpatrick singled to left-field driving in Pat Kelly and tying the score at two. The game would remain tied until the top of the tenth when Royals third baseman Paul Schaal led off the inning with a home run to left giving the Royals a 3-2 lead. Not ready to go home quite yet, the Brewers tied the game in the bottom of the inning on Mike Hegan's run-scoring single to knot the game at 3-3. Dick Ellsworth would come in and pitch the 11th, setting the Royals down in order, giving way to Ken Sanders in the twelfth who pitched two three up three down innings. Finally in the bottom of the thirteenth Dave May would lead off with a single and move to second on Ted Savage's bunt single. Bernie Smith would sacrifice the runners over and Royals reliever Tom Burgmeier would issue an intentional walk to Gus Gil. Jerry Mc Nertney hit a hard grounder to shortstop Rich Severson who threw home for the force-out on May. The Royals would go to their relief ace Ted Abernathy the face Ted Kubiak. Kubiak would come through as he laced a single to left field scoring Savage and giving the Brewers a walk-off 4-3 victory in game one of the series.

Although game two of the series lacked the excitement of the previous night, once again the Brewers would come out on top with a 4-3 victory. The Royals would score first in the top of the first inning on an RBI double by Bob Oliver, but the Brewers would come back in their half of the inning as an error by third baseman Paul Schaal allowed Tommy Harper to score on Ted Savage's ground ball. Roberto Pena singled to center driving in

Savage and Dave May. Ted Kubiak singled the right field scoring Pena and giving the Brewers a 4-1 lead, a lead they would never relinquish. Al Downing pitched well, and for once he received run support from the offense as he scattered four hits over 6 and 1/3 innings. With relief help from Dick Ellsworth, and Ken Sanders, who registered his ninth save of the season, Downing picked up his fifth victory.

Kansas City pitchers Wally Bunker and Ted Abernathy handcuffed the Brewers on just three hits taking game three, 4 - 1. The only Brewers offense came on an RBI walk to Ted Savage in the bottom of the eighth, as the Brewers winning streak ended at two. A crowd of 12,562 came out and a cool Saturday evening and with only four home games left in the season the Brewers were still giving them their money's worth.

The Brewers wrapped up the series with the Royals with a Sunday afternoon tilt, and although they were up against the season opener for the Green Bay Packers, 12,841 faithful still showed up at the ballpark and saw another exciting game from their Brewers. The Brewers scored first in the bottom of the first inning on a run-scoring sacrifice by Ted Savage. Brewers' starter Skip Lockwood pitched well holding the Royals scoreless through five innings. In the bottom of the fifth inning Tommy Harper tripled to left field scoring Phil Roof. After a Mike Hegan walk, and with Dave May at the plate, Hegan faked a steal to second base, allowing himself to get caught in a rundown. While the Royals were paying attention to Hegan, Harper broke for home, stealing the base standing up giving the Brewers' third run of the game. The Brewers picked up another run in the bottom of the sixth as Phil Roof executed a perfect suicide-squeeze, scoring Russ Snyder and running the Brewers' lead to 4-0. The Royals would finally get to Lockwood in the top of the seventh, scoring three runs before Ken Sanders came out of the bullpen and shut down the Royals' rally. Sanders was perfect the rest of the way and the Brewers held on for an exciting 4-3 victory and a series win versus the Royals. With the victory the Brewers were now one game out of fourth place in the American League Western Division. Lockwood pitched well, going six innings giving up three runs and three hits, and Sanders pitched the final three, giving up two hits and earning his 10th save of the season.

The Brewers opened up their final home series of the 1970 season with a three-game match up against the California Angels. A crowd of only 4,891 turned out on an unseasonably warm Monday evening and saw the Brewers and Angels engage in a seesaw affair. The Angels got on the board first on back-to-back RBI singles by Roger Repoz and Joe Azcue to take a 2-0 lead. The Brewers took the lead back in the bottom of the fourth inning on Phil Roof's 13th home run of the season, a three-run shot off of Angel starter Tom Murphy. The Angels would get to Brewers starter Lew Krausse in the top of the seventh when pinch hitter Jay Johnstone took Krausse deep to right field for a two-run home run, and two batters later the Murphy hit one over the left-field fence, making the score 5-3. The Brewers would get a run back on Tommy Harper's 28th home run of the season to bring the Brewers within one. After giving up back-to-back singles to open the eighth, Krause was replaced by Dick Ellsworth, and Ellsworth's second batter, Roger Repoz tripled to center field scoring Alex Johnson and Jim Fregosi making the score 7-5. John Gelnar replaced Ellsworth and recorded the last two outs of the inning. The score would hold until the bottom of the ninth inning when Tommy Harper hit his second home run of the game and 29th of the season, a two-run shot deep to center field making the score 7-6. That's as close as the Brewers would get as Angels' reliever Eddie Fisher got the next three batters all on ground outs and the Brewers dropped a one-run decision 7-6.

Despite of a strong outing in game two from Marty Pattin it took some late inning heroics for the Brewers to even up the series with the Angels. Pattin would go seven innings giving up only three hits, one of those a solo shot from Jim Fregosi in the third inning giving the Angels a 2-0 lead. Angels' starter

Rudy May pitched well, holding the Brewers scoreless until the bottom of the seventh inning. After giving up back-to-back singles to Phil Roof and Mike Hegan, Angels' manager Lefty Phillips went to his bullpen, bringing in Dave La Roche to face Ted Kubiak. Kubiak grounded into a fielder's choice allowing pinch-runner Max Alvis to score, bringing the Brewers within one run. La Roche would get Jerry Mc Nertney to pop out and Phillips once again went to his bullpen, this time bringing in Mel Queen. Tommy Harper would make Phillips and the Angels pay as he crushed a long home run to left field scoring Ted Kubiak and giving the Brewers a 3-2 lead. Queen would plunk the next batter Bernie Smith bringing up Dave May. May lashed a double to right field scoring Smith giving the Brewers a 4-2 lead. Ken Sanders came in from the bullpen and tossed two scoreless innings earning his eleventh save of the season as the Brewers downed the Angels 4-2. Starting pitcher Marty Pattin continued his late-season surge and with the victory ran his record to 13-12 for the season and lowering his ERA to 3.45.

The 5,795 fans that showed up on that Tuesday night saw history made as Tommy Harper's seventh inning home run was his 30th on the season, making him only the fifth player in Major League history to have 30 home runs and at least 30 stolen bases in the same season. Harper was going into the last week of the season with a legitimate opportunity to capture the American League MVP Award with his performance.

Mother Nature took one more swipe at the Brewers as after a 1 hour and 30 minute rain delay Wednesday's series finale was postponed and rescheduled for Thursday afternoon. A crowd of 6,549 showed up for the afternoon game to catch their Brewers one more time during the 1970 season, and the Brewers did not disappoint. The Brewers' offense got started early as Tommy Harper led off the bottom of the first inning with his 31st home run of the year to deep left field. Dave May doubled to left and the next batter, Ted Savage, would poke a single to right field scoring May giving the Brewers a 2-0 lead. The Brewers would add on in the bottom of the second inning on a run-scoring single from Tommy Harper and a run-scoring single from Mike Hegan. After an intentional walk to Dave May, Ted Savage singled to left scoring Hegan and Harper, giving the Brewers a 6-0 lead. The Brewers would tally their seventh run on a run-scoring single from Ted Savage in the fourth, while starter John Morris held the Angels scoreless through five. The Angels would finally get to Morris in the fifth on a run-scoring double from Jarvis Tatum, and run-scoring singles from Billy Cowan, and Chico Ruiz. John Gelnar would come in from the pen and throw a scoreless 7th and 8th innings, and Ken Sanders would work around two 9th inning singles to shut the door as the Brewers won their last home game of the 1970 season, 7-3. Starter John Morris earned the victory to even in his record at 3-3, while Sanders picked up his 12th save of the season.

Although the Brewers would fall just short in their quest to draw one million fans, the club, ownership, and fans had to be thrilled with the turnout and support that the Brewers received that first year in Milwaukee. The club would finish the season with 933,690 paid admissions, an improvement of almost 300,000 over the prior year when the club was based in Seattle. Considering the fact that the Brewers had no offseason to promote the team or sell season tickets the attendance figures showed without a doubt that the city of Milwaukee deserved Major League Baseball, and would come out to support their team.

The Brewers set out on their final road trip of the season starting with a Friday night doubleheader against the White Sox. White Sox lefty Tommy John held the Brewers to one run and seven hits over nine innings as the White Sox built a 5-0 lead by the bottom of the fifth. The only offense the Brewers could muster came in the ninth inning when Pete Koegel hit his first major league home run with two outs in the top of the ninth inning. Brewers' starter Skip Lockwood would go seven innings giving up five runs on nine hits before giving way to Baldwin and Ellsworth out of the bullpen.

The Brewers would come back and win game two, an exciting 3-2 victory. Surprise starter Bob Humphreys went five innings giving up one earned run while Dick Ellsworth came in out of the bullpen pitching the last 3 and 1/3 innings earning his third save of the season. The game was scoreless until the top of the fourth when Mike Hegan singled to center, and scored on a Jerry Mc Nertney single. The next batter, Roberto Pena doubled to right field scoring Mc Nertney giving the Brewers a 2-0 lead. Bob Burda's sacrifice in the top of the fifth ran the score to 3-0 before the White Sox got on the board on a Bill Melton sacrifice in the bottom of the fifth. John Gelnar would come on in relief in the bottom of the sixth and the first batter, Rich McKinney, would take Gelnar deep, making the score 3-2. After loading the bases, Bristol would summon Dick Ellsworth from the bullpen to end the inning. Ellsworth would retire the side the rest of the way, giving the Brewers a 3-2 victory and a split of the doubleheader.

Game three of the series was a reminder of why the White Sox were considering abandoning the South Side, as a crowd of only 1,602 showed up for a Saturday afternoon game at White Sox Park. The game was delayed for 30 minutes as the grounds crew was having some issues with the grooming of the field. When the game did start, the sparse crowd witnessed a 12-inning affair between the Brewers and the White Sox as the bullpens kept both teams in the game. Starter Lew Krausse lasted 4 and 2/3 innings, giving up four runs on six hits, while White Sox' starter Floyd Weaver was pulled in the fifth inning, also having given up four runs. The game would stay tied at five until the top of the 12th when the Brewers' offense erupted for four runs off of two White Sox relievers. Singles by Hegan and Mc Nertney, and an intentional walk to Kubiak loaded the bases. Bristol sent Gus Gil to pinch-hit for Russ Snyder and Gil walked scoring Hegan. Tommy Harper singled to left driving in McNerney and Kubiak. Harper was caught stealing second but Bernie Smith singled to third, scoring Gus Gil and giving the Brewers a 9-5 lead. Gene Brabender would come in and pitch the ninth retiring the White Sox in order to register his first save of the year as the Brewers took a 9-5 victory.

The Brewers wrapped up their season series with the White Sox in front of another cozy gathering of around 3,000 by pounding out 15 hits in a 9-3 decision. White Sox' starter Joe Horlen handcuffed the Brewers through six innings, taking a 1-0 lead into the top of the seventh. The Brewers offense would explode for seven runs in the inning, the longest hit being a single. Tito Francona started the scoring with a run-scoring single to center and the next batter, Ted Kubiak singled to left scoring Roberto Pena and Francona. Pattin would help his own cause as he laid down a bunt single scoring Kubiak. After getting Bernie Smith to ground into a fielder's choice, Dave May singled to right scoring Max Alvis. Ted Savage drew walk and Mike Hegan singled to right scoring Smith and May and turning a close game into a 7-1 blowout for the Brewers. The Brewers tacked on two more in the top of the ninth on a two-run single from Mike Hegan. Pattin would give up two in the bottom of the ninth, but shut the White Sox down giving the Brewers a 9-3 victory and the series win. Pattin would go the distance giving up three runs while scattering seven hits to run his season record to 14 - 12. Although Pattin started the year slowly, he pitched well in the second half and was becoming the workhorse of the Brewers' rotation.

The Brewers headed west to wrap up the season with a three-game series against the Oakland A's. The Brewers only needed to take one game out of the series to guarantee their first winning month of the season. They had already surpassed the Pilots' win total from 1969 and were looking to add on. The Brewers would face Oakland's Jim "Catfish" Hunter in game one and after falling behind 2-0 the Brewers were unable to take the lead against Hunter. They would get as close as 4-3 with one run of the top of the eighth inning, but Hunter would go the distance striking out ten, and scattering nine hits, one of them Ted Savage's 12th home run of the season. Al

Downing started for the Brewers and was lifted with two outs in the fourth inning after having giving up six runs, while the bullpen combo of John Morris and Ken Sanders kept Oakland scoreless the rest of the way.

The Brewers penultimate game of the 1970 season would be played before 2,302 fans at the cavernous Oakland-Alameda County Coliseum. The Brewers would jump on Oakland starter Blue Moon Odom early on a run-scoring single by Mike Hegan. In the top of the third the Brewers tacked on two more on a Ted Savage sacrifice fly and Bob Burda's run-scoring single. Skip Lockwood pitched scoreless ball until the seventh inning when Oakland's Bobby Brooks singled driving in Sal Bando, getting Oakland on the board. The Brewers tacked on one more in the top of the ninth on a run-scoring single from Ted Savage while Ken Sanders pitched two scoreless innings wrapping up the game for the Brewers, giving them a 4-1 victory. Lockwood went 6 and 1/3 innings to earn his fifth win of the season and Sanders registered his 13th save. More importantly with the victory, the Brewers had secured their first winning month in franchise history and showed the steady improvement evident throughout the season.

Although it was the final day of the season, the Brewers front office was not done. Earlier in the day they announced they had signed amateur free-agent outfielder Sixto Lezcano. The seventeen-year-old Lezcano, a native of Puerto Rico was considered a fine prospect, and although nobody could have guessed at the time, he would play major a role in the Brewers' future success

The Brewers closed out the 1970 season with a heartbreaking 5-4 loss to the Oakland A's. The game was tied at one until the top of the sixth inning when, with Roberto Pena at the plate, Dave May took off for home, stealing the base giving the Brewers a 2-1 lead. In the top of the seventh, Tommy Harper doubled scoring Marty Pattin and Mike Hegan putting the Brewers up 4-1. Oakland would come back in the bottom of the 8th on a two-run home run from Bobby Brooks and Pattin was lifted for Ken Sanders. The Brewers would take a 4-3 lead into the bottom of the ninth inning when Reggie Jackson doubled, scoring Sal Bando and Joe Rudi to give the A's a 5-4 come-from-behind victory wrapping up the 1970 season for the Brewers.

The Brewers would finish the season with 65 wins and 97 losses, good for fourth place in the American League Western Division. The team had drawn close to 1 million fans and played an exciting brand of baseball, while showing continued improvement. Like any second-year team there were ups and downs, but the organization had strong leadership not only in the front office, but on the field and with the coaching staff and there was reason for optimism for the future of baseball in the City of Milwaukee. Regardless of the club's record, the fans not only in Milwaukee but throughout the entire state had taken the Brewers to heart and once again had a team to call their own. They were definitely big-league again!

EPILOGUE

The Brewers' first season in Milwaukee may not have been a success in the standings, but it was a success in the stands and in the community. Almost one million fans went through the turnstiles, once again breathing life into Milwaukee County Stadium. The club finished seventh in the American League in attendance out drawing established teams such as the Senators, Indians, and Athletics, and almost doubling the White Sox' home attendance for the season.

The city's enthusiasm for the team was certainly evident to the players, and their enthusiasm for the fans was just a strong. *"The move was energizing,"* said Ted Kubiak *"how could it not be, going to an old established baseball town like Milwaukee. I loved the city; we lived in Waukesha with some of the other families. I loved my snowmobile in the winter, and hated to sell it when we came back to California. The fans were great, and glad to have a team again thanks to Bud Selig."* Catcher Phil Roof echoed that sentiment, *"The baseball fan base there was hungry for Major League Baseball again. I have great respect for Bud Selig for his leadership and commitment to bringing Major League Baseball back to Milwaukee. They (the fans) treated us with respect and were very excited to have a major league team back in town to call their own"*

On the field, the biggest highlight was Tommy Harper and the season that he put together. In 1969, Harper would lead the league in stolen bases with 73, but only produced nine home runs and a 235 batting average. In 1970 Harper crushed a career-high 31 home runs while still adding 38 stolen bases and raising his batting average 61 points. Although Harper finished 6th in the MVP voting many people, including some teammates, thought he should have been the league MVP. Pitcher Dave Baldwin said, *"Tommy Harper was outstanding that season - he should have been the league's MVP."*

Harper wasn't the only highlight on the field for the Brewers that season. Spring training sensation Danny Walton became one of the fans' first heroes and had a breakout season hitting 17 home runs along with 66 RBIs. Had a late season injury not sidelined Walton, those numbers certainly would have been higher. The catching duo of Roof and Mc Nertney combined for 19 home runs in 59 RBIs and gave the Brewers solid defense behind the plate. The biggest improvement showed in the bullpen as a series of call ups and mid-season acquisitions give the Brewers one of the strongest relief corps in baseball. The May promotions of Dave Baldwin and Ken Sanders helped solidify the bullpen, with Sanders pitching himself into the role of closer and earning the nickname the "Bulldog". There's no question that the veteran influence in the bullpen and their solid pitching played a major role in the club's strong showing in the month of September.

Milwaukee had once again been established as a major league city, and once the excitement of that first-year had faded, it was time to look to the future. There would be changes, and there would be struggles, and for the good part of the 1970s, the Brewers would not play winning baseball.

Nevertheless they were accumulating young talent and some of the players in their minor league system showed promise and would be promoted to the big club. Two of them, Gorman Thomas and pitcher Bill Travers would be key players in the club's transformation into a winner. In the 1973 June draft the Brewers had the number three overall pick and drafted a 17 year old shortstop out of Taft High School in Woodland Hills, California. The following year as an 18 year old, Robin Yount would make his debut with the Brewers and for the next 20 seasons would be the face of the franchise, culminating with his induction into the Baseball Hall of Fame.

Although attendance would drop off in '71 and '72, the 1973 season saw the Brewers break the one million mark in attendance for the first time. They would fall just short of the one million mark in 1974, but they would draw more than one million fans every non-strike year since. 1975 saw former Milwaukee Braves' hero Hank Aaron return to Milwaukee and play the last two years of his career with the Brewers. The team's fortunes would begin to change when Orioles' pitching coach George Bamberger was hired as manager and in 1978 the Brewers turned in their first winning season as "Bambi's Bombers" took the city by storm. The Brewers were one of the best teams in baseball throughout the late '70s and early '80s, as their freewheeling, fence busting style appealed to the Milwaukee baseball fan. The culmination of that first era of success was their appearance in the 1982 World Series. Although they did not win the series that club led by Harvey Kuenn will always be cherished by Milwaukee baseball fans.

The club's fortunes would be up and down over the next decades as many changes would occur. By the mid-1990s it was painfully obvious that Milwaukee County Stadium was outdated and would need to be replaced to keep Milwaukee viable as a major league city. The fans support and love for the team never wavered, but in order to compete they needed a facility to match the times. Led by the strong-willed efforts of Bud Selig the Brewers were finally able to begin construction of a beautiful retractable roof stadium that would be the envy of Major League Baseball and assure that the Brewers would remain in Milwaukee.

It was through the unyielding and unwavering efforts of Bud Selig that baseball fans in Milwaukee are still cheering their Milwaukee Brewers. Although Mr. Selig no longer owns the club, every baseball fan in Wisconsin owes him a debt of gratitude. County Stadium may be gone, and 50 years may have passed, but we'll never forget those 41 men who took the field that first year for the Milwaukee Brewers as they were our original heroes and paved the way for the heroes we cheer today.

1970 Milwaukee Brewers Roster

#	Pitchers	Height	Weight	Throws	Bats
46	Dave Baldwin	6-02	200	Right	Right
39	Bobby Bolin	6-04	200	Right	Right
32	Gene Brabender	6-05½	225	Right	Right
31	Bruce Brubaker	6-01	198	Right	Right
36	Al Downing	5-11	177	Left	Right
49	Dick Ellsworth	6-04	195	Left	Left
25	John Gelnar	6-01½	190	Right	Right
47	Bob Humphreys	5-11	170	Right	Right
24	Lew Krausse	5-11	186	Right	Right
49	George Lauzerique	6-01	180	Right	Right
23	Bob Locker	6-03	200	Right	Both
42	Skip Lockwood	6-00	190	Right	Right
38	Bob Meyer	6-02	185	Left	Right
35	John Morris	6-01	198	Left	Right
43	John O'Donoghue	6-03	210	Left	Right
33	Marty Pattin	5-11	180	Right	Right
41	Ray Peters	6-06	210	Right	Right
20	Ken Sanders	5-11	185	Right	Right
48	Wayne Twitchell	6-06	220	Right	Right
	Catchers				
15	Jerry McNertney	6-01	195	Right	Right
5	Phil Roof	6-03	210	Right	Right
	Infielders				
10	Max Alvis	5-11	187	Right	Right
9	Tito Francona	5-11	190	Left	Left
16	Gus Gil	5-10	180	Right	Right
34	Greg Goossen	6-01½	210	Right	Right
21	Tommy Harper	5-10	168	Right	Right
8	Mike Hegan	6-01	190	Left	Left
11	John Kennedy	6-00	185	Right	Right
1	Ted Kubiak	6-00	175	Right	Both

28	Roberto Pena	5-08	175	Right	Right
9	Rich Rollins	5-10	185	Right	Right
45	Fred Stanley	5-10	167	Right	Right

Outfielders

44	Hank Allen	6-00	190	Right	Right
19	Bob Burda	5-11	180	Left	Left
20	Wayne Comer	5-10	175	Right	Right
6	Mike Hershberger	5-10	175	Right	Right
36	Steve Hovley	5-10	188	Left	Left
17	Pete Koegel	6-06½	230	Right	Right
11	Dave May	5-10½	186	Right	Left
2	Ted Savage	6-01	185	Right	Right
22	Bernie Smith	5-09	164	Right	Right
7	Russ Snyder	6-01	190	Right	Left
28	Sandy Valdespino	5-08	170	Left	Left
12	Danny Walton	6-00	200	Right	Right
40	Floyd Wicker	6-02	175	Right	Left

1970 Milwaukee Brewers Batting

Name	G	AB	R	H	2B	3B	HR	RBI	AVG
Hank Allen	28	61	4	14	4	0	0	4	.230
Max Alvis	62	115	16	21	2	0	3	12	.183
Dave Baldwin	28	2	0	1	0	0	0	0	.500
Bobby Bolin	32	36	3	7	0	0	1	2	.194
G. Brabender	29	41	1	4	2	0	0	2	.098
Bruce Brubaker	1	0	0	0	0	0	0	0	.000
Bob Burda	78	222	19	55	9	0	4	20	.248
Wayne Comer	13	17	1	1	0	0	0	1	.059
Al Downing	17	24	0	2	0	0	0	1	.083
Dick Ellsworth	14	0	0	0	0	0	0	0	.000
Tito Francona	52	65	4	15	3	0	0	4	.231
John Gelnar	53	12	1	1	0	0	0	0	.083
Gus Gil	64	119	12	22	4	0	1	12	.185
Greg Goossen	21	47	3	12	3	0	1	3	.255
Tommy Harper	154	604	104	179	35	4	31	82	.296
Mike Hegan	148	476	70	116	21	2	11	52	.244
M. Hershberger	49	98	7	23	5	0	1	6	.235
Steve Hovley	40	135	17	38	9	0	0	16	.281
B. Humphreys	23	9	0	0	0	0	0	0	.000
John Kennedy	25	55	8	14	2	0	2	6	.255
Pete Koegel	7	8	2	2	0	0	1	1	.250
Lew Krausse	38	65	3	9	0	1	0	4	.138
Ted Kubiak	158	540	63	136	9	6	4	41	.252
G. Lauzerique	11	10	2	2	0	0	1	4	.200
Bob Locker	28	1	0	0	0	0	0	0	.000
Skip Lockwood	27	53	2	12	1	0	1	2	.226
Dave May	100	342	36	82	8	1	7	31	.240
J. McNertney	111	296	27	72	11	1	6	22	.243
Bob Meyer	10	3	0	1	0	0	0	0	.333

John Morris	20	17	2	3	1	0	0	0	.176
J. O'Donoghue	25	2	0	0	0	0	0	0	.000
Marty Pattin	43	70	4	9	1	0	0	3	.129
Roberto Pena	121	416	36	99	19	1	3	42	.238
Ray Peters	2	0	0	0	0	0	0	0	.000
Rich Rollins	14	25	3	5	1	0	0	5	.200
Phil Roof	110	321	39	73	7	1	13	37	.227
Ken Sanders	50	13	3	3	0	0	0	0	.231
Ted Savage	114	276	43	77	10	5	12	50	.279
Bernie Smith	44	76	8	21	3	1	1	6	.276
Russ Snyder	124	276	34	64	11	0	4	31	.232
Fred Stanley	6	0	1	0	0	0	0	0	.000
W. Twitchell	2	0	0	0	0	0	0	0	.000
S. Valdespino	8	9	0	0	0	0	0	0	.000
Danny Walton	117	397	32	102	20	1	17	66	.257
Floyd Wicker	15	41	3	8	1	0	1	3	.195

1970 Milwaukee Brewers Pitching

Name	G	GS	W	L	ERA	SV	IP	BB	SO
Dave Baldwin	28	0	2	1	2.55	1	35.1	18	26
Bobby Bolin	32	20	5	11	4.91	1	132	67	81
Gene Brabender	29	21	6	15	6.02	1	128	79	76
Bruce Brubaker	1	0	0	0	9.00	0	2	1	0
Al Downing	17	16	2	10	3.34	0	94.1	59	53
Dick Ellsworth	14	0	0	0	1.72	1	15.2	3	9
John Gelnar	53	0	4	3	4.19	4	92.1	23	48
Bob Humphreys	23	1	2	4	3.15	3	45.2	22	32
Lew Krausse	37	35	13	18	4.75	0	216	67	130
G. Lauzerique	11	4	1	2	6.94	0	35	14	24
Bob Locker	28	0	0	1	3.41	3	31.2	10	19
Skip Lockwood	27	26	5	12	4.30	0	173	79	93
Bob Meyer	10	0	0	1	6.38	0	18.1	12	20
John Morris	20	9	4	3	3.93	0	73.1	22	40
J. O'Donoghue	25	0	2	0	5.01	0	23.1	9	13
Marty Pattin	37	29	14	12	3.39	0	233	71	161
Ray Peters	2	2	0	2	31.50	0	2	5	1
Ken Sanders	50	0	5	2	1.75	13	92.1	25	64
Wayne Twitchell	2	0	0	0	10.80	0	1.2	1	5

1970 Splits

Month (Games)	Won	Lost	WP
April (20)	5	15	0.250
May (26)	10	15	0.400
June (29)	11	18	0.379
July (30)	12	18	0.400
August (29)	12	17	0.414
September (28)	15	13	0.536
October (1)	0	1	0.000

Team vs Team Splits

Opponent (Games)	Won	Lost	WP
Baltimore Orioles (12)	5	7	0.417
Boston Red Sox (12)	7	5	0.583
California Angels (18)	6	12	0.333
Chicago White Sox (18)	11	7	0.611
Cleveland Indians (12)	5	7	0.417
Detroit Tigers (12)	4	8	0.333
Kansas City Royals (18)	6	12	0.333
Minnesota Twins (18)	5	13	0.278
New York Yankees (13)	3	9	0.250
Oakland Athletics (18)	8	10	0.444
Washington Senators (12)	5	7	0.417

Score Related Splits

Type (Games)	Won	Lost	WP
Shutouts (13)	2	11	0.154
1-Run Games (61)	28	33	0.459
Blowouts (26)	6	20	0.231

1970 Milwaukee Brewers Game Results

	Date		Opp	W/L	R	RA	Inn	W-L
1	Tuesday, Apr 7		CAL	L	0	12		0-1
2	Wednesday, Apr 8		CAL	L	1	6		0-2
3	Friday, Apr 10	@	CHW	L	4	5		0-3
4	Saturday, Apr 11	@	CHW	W	8	4		1-3
5	Sunday, Apr 12 (1)	@	CHW	W	5	2		2-3
6	Sunday, Apr 12 (2)	@	CHW	W	16	2		3-3
7	Monday, Apr 13	@	OAK	L	1	2		3-4
8	Tuesday, Apr 14	@	OAK	L	1	9		3-5
9	Thursday, Apr 16		KCR	L	6	8		3-6
10	Saturday, Apr 18		CHW	L	5	8		3-7
11	Monday, Apr 20	@	CAL	L-wo	4	5	10	3-8
12	Tuesday, Apr 21	@	CAL	L	1	3		3-9
13	Wednesday, Apr 22	@	CAL	L	1	3		3-10
14	Saturday, Apr 25 (1)	@	BOS	W	10	4		4-10
15	Saturday, Apr 25 (2)	@	BOS	L	0	3		4-11
16	Sunday, Apr 26	@	BOS	W	5	3		5-11
17	Monday, Apr 27	@	WSA	L-wo	5	6	10	5-12
18	Tuesday, Apr 28	@	WSA	L	6	9		5-13
19	Wednesday, Apr 29	@	WSA	L	0	4		5-14
20	Thursday, Apr 30	@	WSA	L	2	12		5-15
21	Friday, May 1	@	NYY	L	3	6		5-16
22	Saturday, May 2	@	NYY	L-wo	6	7		5-17
23	Sunday, May 3 (1)	@	NYY	L	7	8		5-18
24	Sunday, May 3 (2)	@	NYY	L	2	4		5-19
25	Tuesday, May 5		BOS	L	0	6		5-20
26	Wednesday, May 6		BOS	W	4	3		6-20
27	Thursday, May 7		BOS	W	5	1		7-20

28	Saturday, May 9		WSA	W-wo	3	2	10	8-20
29	Sunday, May 10 (1)		WSA	W-wo	6	5		9-20
30	Sunday, May 10 (2)		WSA	W-wo	7	6		10-20
31	Monday, May 11		NYY	T	5	5		10-20
32	Tuesday, May 12		NYY	L	5	9		10-21
33	Wednesday, May 13		NYY	W	3	1		11-21
34	Saturday, May 16		MIN	L	7	11		11-22
35	Sunday, May 17		MIN	L	1	6		11-23
36	Tuesday, May 19		OAK	W	6	3		12-23
37	Wednesday, May 20		OAK	W-wo	8	7		13-23
38	Friday, May 22	@	KCR	L	3	6		13-24
39	Saturday, May 23	@	KCR	L	1	3		13-25
40	Sunday, May 24	@	KCR	L-wo	5	6	10	13-26
41	Monday, May 25	@	MIN	L	5	6		13-27
42	Tuesday, May 26	@	MIN	L	2	6		13-28
43	Thursday, May 28	@	MIN	L	2	11		13-29
44	Friday, May 29		DET	L	4	5		13-30
45	Saturday, May 30		DET	W	9	7		14-30
46	Sunday, May 31		DET	W-wo	7	6		15-30
47	Tuesday, Jun 2 (1)		CLE	L	1	4		15-31
48	Tuesday, Jun 2 (2)		CLE	L	5	9		15-32
49	Wednesday, Jun 3		CLE	L	6	7		15-33
50	Thursday, Jun 4		CLE	L	4	8		15-34
51	Friday, Jun 5		BAL	L	2	3		15-35
52	Saturday, Jun 6		BAL	W	6	4		16-35
53	Sunday, Jun 7		BAL	L	6	7		16-36
54	Monday, Jun 8		CHW	W	5	2		17-36
55	Tuesday, Jun 9	@	DET	L	3	8		17-37
56	Wednesday, Jun 10	@	DET	L	5	7		17-38
57	Thursday, Jun 11	@	DET	L	2	6		17-39
58	Friday, Jun 12	@	CLE	W	4	1		18-39
59	Saturday, Jun 13	@	CLE	L	6	10		18-40

60	Sunday, Jun 14	@	CLE	L	2	9		18-41
61	Monday, Jun 15	@	BAL	W	9	6		19-41
62	Wednesday, Jun 17	@	BAL	W	5	1		20-41
63	Friday, Jun 19	@	CAL	W	5	2		21-41
64	Saturday, Jun 20	@	CAL	L	0	4		21-42
65	Sunday, Jun 21	@	CAL	L-wo	5	6	10	21-43
66	Monday, Jun 22		MIN	L	3	4		21-44
67	Tuesday, Jun 23		MIN	W-wo	4	3		22-44
68	Wednesday, Jun 24		MIN	L	2	3		22-45
69	Thursday, Jun 25		MIN	W	4	1		23-45
70	Friday, Jun 26		OAK	W-wo	3	2	15	24-45
71	Saturday, Jun 27		OAK	W	3	1		25-45
72	Sunday, Jun 28 (1)		OAK	L	1	4		25-46
73	Sunday, Jun 28 (2)		OAK	L	1	4		25-47
74	Monday, Jun 29		CAL	L	3	10		25-48
75	Tuesday, Jun 30		CAL	W	5	4		26-48
76	Wednesday, Jul 1		CAL	L	3	4		26-49
77	Thursday, Jul 2		CAL	L	7	10		26-50
78	Friday, Jul 3 (1)		KCR	L	3	5	10	26-51
79	Friday, Jul 3 (2)		KCR	L	3	4		26-52
80	Saturday, Jul 4		KCR	L	6	8		26-53
81	Sunday, Jul 5		KCR	W	2	1		27-53
82	Monday, Jul 6		CHW	W	3	1		28-53
83	Tuesday, Jul 7 (1)		CHW	W-wo	4	3	12	29-53
84	Tuesday, Jul 7 (2)		CHW	W	1	0		30-53
85	Wednesday, Jul 8		CHW	L	1	2		30-54
86	Thursday, Jul 9		CHW	L	5	6		30-55
87	Friday, Jul 10	@	OAK	W	2	1		31-55
88	Saturday, Jul 11	@	OAK	L	1	11		31-56
89	Sunday, Jul 12 (1)	@	OAK	L-wo	3	4		31-57
90	Sunday, Jul 12 (2)	@	OAK	W	2	1		32-57
91	Thursday, Jul 16	@	BOS	L-wo	5	6	10	32-58

92	Friday, Jul 17	@	BOS	L	2	8		32-59
93	Saturday, Jul 18	@	BOS	W	10	5		33-59
94	Sunday, Jul 19	@	WSA	L-wo	3	4		33-60
95	Monday, Jul 20	@	WSA	L	0	2		33-61
96	Tuesday, Jul 21	@	NYY	L	2	4		33-62
97	Wednesday, Jul 22	@	NYY	W	4	1		34-62
98	Friday, Jul 24		BOS	W	8	4		35-62
99	Saturday, Jul 25		BOS	W	6	2		36-62
100	Sunday, Jul 26		BOS	L	5	12		36-63
101	Tuesday, Jul 28		WSA	W	5	1		37-63
102	Wednesday, Jul 29		WSA	L	2	4		37-64
103	Thursday, Jul 30		WSA	W	6	2		38-64
104	Friday, Jul 31 (1)		NYY	L	3	7		38-65
105	Friday, Jul 31 (2)		NYY	L	3	5		38-66
106	Saturday, Aug 1		NYY	L	1	4	12	38-67
107	Sunday, Aug 2		NYY	W	9	5		39-67
108	Monday, Aug 3 (1)	@	MIN	L	1	2		39-68
109	Monday, Aug 3 (2)	@	MIN	W	4	2		40-68
110	Tuesday, Aug 4	@	MIN	L	2	5		40-69
111	Wednesday, Aug 5	@	CHW	L	3	9		40-70
112	Thursday, Aug 6	@	CHW	L	3	7		40-71
113	Friday, Aug 7 (1)	@	KCR	L	0	4		40-72
114	Friday, Aug 7 (2)	@	KCR	L	2	10		40-73
115	Saturday, Aug 8	@	KCR	W	5	3		41-73
116	Sunday, Aug 9	@	KCR	W	4	2		42-73
117	Tuesday, Aug 11		DET	L	1	2		42-74
118	Wednesday, Aug 12		DET	W	6	5		43-74
119	Thursday, Aug 13		DET	W	3	2		44-74
120	Friday, Aug 14		CLE	W-wo	4	3	11	45-74
121	Sunday, Aug 16		CLE	W-wo	4	3		46-74
122	Monday, Aug 17		BAL	L	2	3		46-75
123	Tuesday, Aug 18		BAL	L	0	3		46-76

124	Wednesday, Aug 19		BAL	L	2	3		46-77
125	Friday, Aug 21	@	DET	L	4	6		46-78
126	Saturday, Aug 22	@	DET	L	2	5		46-79
127	Sunday, Aug 23	@	DET	L	0	1		46-80
128	Tuesday, Aug 25	@	CLE	W	4	2	10	47-80
129	Wednesday, Aug 26	@	CLE	L	2	7		47-81
130	Thursday, Aug 27	@	CLE	W	14	2		48-81
131	Friday, Aug 28 (1)	@	BAL	W	2	1		49-81
132	Friday, Aug 28 (2)	@	BAL	L	4	8		49-82
133	Saturday, Aug 29	@	BAL	L	1	6		49-83
134	Sunday, Aug 30	@	BAL	W	5	2		50-83
135	Tuesday, Sep 1 (1)		MIN	L	0	4		50-84
136	Tuesday, Sep 1 (2)		MIN	L	1	7	11	50-85
137	Thursday, Sep 3		MIN	W	8	3		51-85
138	Friday, Sep 4		CHW	W-wo	3	2	10	52-85
139	Monday, Sep 7 (1)	@	MIN	L	6	7		52-86
140	Monday, Sep 7 (2)	@	MIN	L	3	8		52-87
141	Tuesday, Sep 8	@	MIN	W	3	2		53-87
142	Thursday, Sep 10 (1)	@	KCR	L	0	2		53-88
143	Thursday, Sep 10 (2)	@	KCR	L	2	10		53-89
144	Friday, Sep 11	@	CAL	W	2	1		54-89
145	Saturday, Sep 12	@	CAL	W	3	2		55-89
146	Sunday, Sep 13	@	CAL	L	1	2		55-90
147	Tuesday, Sep 15 (1)		OAK	W	1	0		56-90
148	Tuesday, Sep 15 (2)		OAK	L	5	6		56-91
149	Wednesday, Sep 16		OAK	L	1	4		56-92
150	Thursday, Sep 17		KCR	W-wo	4	3	13	57-92
151	Friday, Sep 18		KCR	W	4	3		58-92
152	Saturday, Sep 19		KCR	L	1	4		58-93
153	Sunday, Sep 20		KCR	W	4	3		59-93
154	Monday, Sep 21		CAL	L	6	7		59-94
155	Tuesday, Sep 22		CAL	W	4	2		60-94

156	Thursday, Sep 24		CAL	W	7	3		61-94
157	Friday, Sep 25 (1)	@	CHW	L	1	5		61-95
158	Friday, Sep 25 (2)	@	CHW	W	3	2		62-95
159	Saturday, Sep 26	@	CHW	W	9	5	12	63-95
160	Sunday, Sep 27	@	CHW	W	9	3		64-95
161	Tuesday, Sep 29	@	OAK	L	3	4		64-96
162	Wednesday, Sep 30	@	OAK	W	4	1		65-96
163	Thursday, Oct 1	@	OAK	L-wo	4	5		65-97

References

(n.d.). Retrieved 2020, from Newspapers.com: www.newspapers.com

(n.d.). Retrieved 2019-2020, from Weather Underground: https://www.wunderground.com/history/daily/us/wi/milwaukee/KMKE

"Bernie Brewer Ends Long Scoreboard Stay". (1970, August 17). *Green Bay Press Gazette*, p. 19.

"Brewer Hopeful Auerbach Hurt". (1970, August 29). *Green Bay Press Gazette"*, p. 9.

"Brewers Draft Catcher Porter". (1970, June 5th). *Green Bay Press Gazette*, p. 14.

"Brewers Lose Long Ball War, Put Hovley on Block". (1970, June 7). *Green Bay Press Gazette*, p. 17.

"Brewers Top Sox On May's Homer...". (1970, July 1). *Green Bay Press Gazette*, pp. B-1.

"Brewers, Royals Even Teams, Schultz Says:Twin-Bill Set". (1970, September 10). *Green Bay Press Gazette*, p. 25.

"Brews Invite Braves for Game". (1970, April 16). *Green Bay Press Gazette*, p. 25.

"Brews Purchase Pitcher Ellsworth". (1970, August 7). *Green Bay Press Gazette*, p. 13.

"Humphreys,Three Others To Rejoin Brews Next Week".
(1970, August 25). *Green Bay Press Gazette*, p. 19.

"Indians Bomb Brewers Behind Hargan, Foster". (1970,
August 27). *Green Bay Press Gazette*, p. 23.

"Old Formula For Brews: Close But Lose". (1970, May 30).
Green Bay Press Gazette, pp. B-1.

"Rumor Brews To Make Deal For Howard". (1970, July
16). *Green Bay Press Gazette*, p. 17.

"They're All Good Guys As Brews Tip Braves,1-0". (1970,
May 15). *Green Bay Press Gazette*, pp. B-1.

Baseball Reference. (n.d.). Retrieved 2019-2020, from
www.baseball-reference.com

Bouton, J. (1970). *Ball Four*. North Engremont: Bulldog
Publishing.

Index

Caguas Criollos, 46

California Angels, 18, 23, 60, 73, 80, 160, 176, 262, 286

Carl Koonce, 196

Carl Yastrzemski, 195, 200

Carlos May, 88, 94, 95, 97, 186, 215, 246

Casey Stengel, 6, 7

Charles O. Finley, 2, 15, 102

Charlie Grimm, 6, 7

Chicago Bears, 86, 157, 224

Chicago Cubs, 6, 29

Chicago Daily News, 38

Chicago White Sox, 8, 23, 26, 45, 57, 75, 105, 163, 286

Chico Ruiz, 252, 266

Chico Salmon, 238

Chuck Dobson, 176, 190

Cincinnati Bengals, 86, 247

Cincinnati Reds, 40, 66

City of Milwaukee, 4, 5, 10, 27, 67, 71, 274

City of Seattle, 23, 47

Cleveland Indians, 7, 16, 23, 28, 63, 65, 155, 157, 193, 215, 286

Clinton Pilots, 45

Clyde Wright, 73, 108

Comiskey Park, 29

Connie Mack, 5

County Stadium, 11, 13, 14, 26, 30, 31, 38, 68, 72, 86, 101, 105, 109, 121, 122, 123, 127, 157, 184, 224, 230, 258, 280

Curt Blefary, 206

Curt Rayer, 154

Cy Young Award, 218, 221

Dan O'Neill, 58

Danny Cater, 118, 138, 206, 210

Danny Murphy, 246

Danny Thompson, 213, 245

Danny Walton, 63, 68, 71, 82, 84, 89, 90, 91, 92, 94, 96, 97, 98, 99, 100, 107, 112, 114, 115, 116, 121, 122, 124, 126, 127, 129, 131, 132, 134,

194, 197, 205, 206, 209, 217, 220, 234, 240, 245, 246, 249, 251, 256, 258, 260, 261, 264, 266, 272, 274, 277, 281, 284, 285

King County Superior Court, 49

Kingdome, *18, 37*

Ladies Day, 101

Lamar Hunt, 37, 42

Lee Maye, 133, 197, 205

Leo Cardenas, 243

Leo Durocher, 29

Lew Alcindor, 58

Lew Krausse, 44, 64, 70, 74, 92, 105, 110, 118, 121, 139, 143, 149, 158, 164, 167, 171, 174, 177, 183, 187, 190, 196, 199, 203, 213, 216, 220, 228, 231, 236, 243, 248, 251, 262, 269, 281, 283, 285

Lindy McDaniel, 116, 119, 206, 210

Lou Perini, 10, 58

Lou Piniella, 184, 258

Luis Aparicio, 88, 93, 186

Luis Tiant, 151, 213, 248

Major League Baseball, 1, 2, 11, 14, 16, 17, 18, 20, 22, 23, 27, 30, 33, 36, 41, 44, 56, 64, 71, 72, 75, 79, 80, 101, 122, 192, 230, 267, 275, 280

Marquette Warriors, 58

Marty Pattin, 51, 60, 70, 81, 112, 115, 131, 133, 146, 148, 167, 171, 173, 177, 182, 186, 190, 197, 200, 204, 212, 217, 221, 222, 223, 228, 232, 237, 245, 249, 253, 258, 263, 273, 281, 284, 285

Marvin Milkes, 18, 40, 50, 101, 108, 120, 163, 178, 194

Max Alvis, 65, 70, 74, 77, 90, 93, 95, 97, 139, 143, 214, 225, 244, 264, 270, 281, 283

Mayo Smith, 232

Mel Stottlemyre, 137, 209

Merle Harmon, 57

Merv Rettenmund, 228, 238

Metropolitan Milwaukee

WTMJ, 58

CPSIA information can be obtained
at www.ICGtesting.com
Printed in the USA
BVHW042154141220
595748BV00020B/352

9 781648 581717